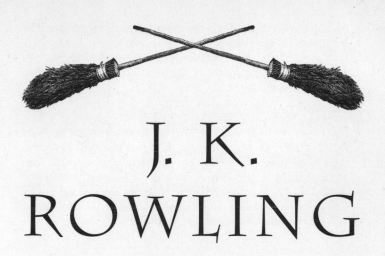

J. K. ROWLING

The Wizard Behind Harry Potter

MARC SHAPIRO

ST. MARTIN'S GRIFFIN

NEW YORK

This Book Is Dedicated to

All the good people. My wife, Nancy. My daughter, Rachael.
My mother, Selma. My agent, Lori. Bennie and Freda. Keri,
Bad Baby, Chaos. Mike Kirby, Steve Ross. And finally to J. K.
Rowling for lighting up the imagination of a whole generation.
All good thoughts to you.

J. K. ROWLING: THE WIZARD BEHIND HARRY POTTER. Copyright
© 2000, 2001 by Marc Shapiro. All rights reserved. Printed in
the United States of America. No part of this book may be used
or reproduced in any manner whatsoever without written per-
mission except in the case of brief quotations embodied in critical
articles or reviews. For information, address St. Martin's Press,
175 Fifth Avenue, New York, N.Y. 10010.

www.stmartins.com

Design by Nancy Resnick

Library of Congress Cataloging-in-Publication Data

Shapiro, Marc.
    J. K. Rowling : the wizard behind Harry Potter / Marc
Shapiro.
        p. cm.
    Includes bibliographical references.
    ISBN 0-312-27224-3
    ISBN 0-312-28662-7 (new and rev.)
    1. Rowling, J. K. 2. Authors, English—20th century—
Biography. 3. Women and literature—England—History—
20th century. 4. Children's stories—Authorship. 5. Potter,
Harry (Fictitious character). I.Title.

PR6068.O93 Z88 2000
823'.914—dc21

                                                      00-031723

First Revised Edition: November 2001

10 9 8 7 6 5 4 3 2 1

SOURCES

Since Harry Potter burst on the scene, J. K. Rowling has been the subject of many press articles and has given many interviews. I found the following publications, with their high level of professionalism, particularly helpful: the Associated Press, *Book*, *The Boston Globe*, *Current Biography*, *Daily Telegraph* (London), *Entertainment Weekly*, *Good Housekeeping*, *The Guardian* (London), *The Hollywood Reporter*, the *Los Angeles Times*, *Maclean's*, *The New York Times*, *Newsweek*, *The Observer* (London), *People*, *Reader's Digest*, *School Library Journal*, *Time*, *Time* (Europe), *Toronto Star*, *Variety*, and *The Washington Post*.

The following Web sites also helped in this journey: J. K. Rowling: Raincoast Kids; Meet J. K. Rowling: Scholastic.com; J. K. Rowling: Bookwire; The Unofficial Harry Potter Fan Club Page; Harry Potter: Scholastic.com; The Essential Harry Potter; books: BBC Online as well as Barnes and Noble.com; CNN.com; The Leaky Cauldron; ICulture; Salon.com; Empireonline; Upcoming Movies.com; Bloomsbury Magazine.com; and CBC.com.

CONTENTS

CONTENTS

INTRODUCTION

I LOVE TO READ

I confess, I love to read.

After a hard day's work, there is no better way to wind down and relax than by curling up in a soft, comfortable chair, putting my feet up on an equally soft stool, and flipping through the pages of a good book as my cat, Chaos, purrs contentedly in my lap. What I read depends on what kind of mood I'm in.

Sometimes I want to find out about real people and real lives, so I will pick up a biography. But there are also those times when reading about the real world is the last thing on my mind. That is when I will pick up a science fiction story, a spooky thriller, or a Harry Potter book . . .

And escape to a place I've never been before.

There has always been a sense of comfort in escaping into a world of fantasy. Which is why the adventures of Harry Potter are so much fun for children and adults alike. There are, quite simply, no rules in a Harry Potter book—or at least none that cannot be broken in the name of fun and adventure.

We can have adventures in the land of Muggle that we cannot have anywhere else. As we flip through the pages of *Harry Potter and the Sorcerer's Stone* or *Harry Potter and the Chamber of Secrets*, we can close our eyes and pretend we've just finished a rousing game of Quidditch and are now back in the hallowed halls of Hogwarts, learning the fine arts of charms, spells, and magic, alongside good friends Ron and Hermione, at the feet of Professor Dumbledore.

Entering the world of Harry Potter is like following Alice down the rabbit hole into Wonderland. It is a place where just about anything can happen and usually does. Some of what goes on is truly frightening. I would not want to meet Voldemort or the Dementor on a dark night. But I sure would love to rip open a Howler and have it scream out its message to me. Traveling by way of Floo Powder would sure beat being stuck in rush-hour traffic. And I doubt anyone could find a better friend than Ron or Hermione.

The sign of a good fantasy is that the reader can lose himself or herself in it. And it goes without saying that millions of children and adults around the world have done just that with the adventures of Harry Potter.

But being curious, we also have questions. How did the author come up with those ideas? What does the person who created Harry look like? What color is her hair? After we have enjoyed our trip to fantasyland, we eventually want to know all about her.

What is the person like who writes Harry Potter stories?

Is she young or old? Happy or sad? Does she live alone, or does she write these fantastic stories with a brood of children underfoot? Did she have a happy childhood or was her family life so unhappy she was driven to escape into the world of fantasy?

Those were the questions I wanted to have answered. Which is why I set out to write *J. K. Rowling: The Wizard Behind Harry Potter*.

Often the story behind the author is as interesting, if not more so, than what is written. In the case of J. K. Rowling, the story has a little bit of everything. There is happiness and love. There is also some sadness. The story of J. K. Rowling is also one of bravery, determination, and triumph over seemingly overwhelming odds.

And finally there is the happy ending. The life of J. K. Rowling sounds very much like the stories she writes and is, in a way, a fairy tale come to life.

Knowing about J. K. Rowling and how she came to write the most popular books in the whole wide world will not change your feelings about Harry Potter. But *J. K. Rowling: The Wizard Behind*

INTRODUCTION

Harry Potter will definitely give you the story behind the story.

And knowing more will only add to the enjoyment the next time you sit in your chair or crawl into bed and pull the covers up tight . . .

And disappear into the land of Harry Potter one more time.

I am back to my comfortable chair and my good book.

Chaos is purring.

It is time to turn the page.

—Marc Shapiro

1

WILD ABOUT HARRY

Sometimes the real world can be a confusing place. It is not always fair or kind. And in the real world there are not always happy endings. Which is why, every once in a while, we like to escape into the world of fantasy—a place where things always go our way and there is always a happy ending.

We want to believe in fantastic creatures in imaginary lands. We want to believe in magic powers, good friends, and the power of good to triumph over evil. We all fantasize about being able to fly and lift buildings off the ground. And how good a magic sword would feel in our hand as we go off to slay a dragon or win the hand of a beautiful princess.

Which is why we like Superman, Peter Pan, Mary Poppins, and the amazing adventures of Frodo in *The Lord of the Rings*. And it is why we are all now Potterites who can't wait for the further adventures of our favorite wizard, Harry Potter, a thirteen-year-old English orphan who attends the Hogwarts School of Witchcraft and Wizardry and tries to be a normal boy while confronting the truly fantastic at every turn.

The author of the Harry Potter books, J. K. (Joanne Kathleen) Rowling, is a grown woman with a child of her own. She is sensible, modest, and realistic—all good qualities when it comes to being a good parent and a positive member of the real world. She likes to walk the streets of her hometown of Edinburgh, Scotland. She will sit for hours at her favorite café, sipping an espresso and watching as the world passes her by.

But there is something that sets J. K. Rowling

apart from the rest of us. For Joanne Kathleen Rowling likes to dream at all hours of the day and night. She dreams of faraway lands, bigger-than-life good guys, truly evil bad guys, and likable young children who try and make sense of it all. But unlike others, she turns her dreams into reality when she sits down with pen and paper and begins to write about the adventures of Harry Potter.

A smile crosses her face. Her already expressive eyes, framed by long wavy hair, grow even wider. Her pen slashes across the paper like a lightning bolt. In her mind, a door to a delightful new world of imagination and wonder has just opened wide and she is about to pass through it.

When J. K. Rowling sits down to give new life to Harry Potter, usually in her favorite writing place, a café called Nicholson's, a change comes over the author. Because to create the latest adventure of Harry, his good friends Ron Weasley and Hermione Granger, and their adventures, Joanne has to stop being an adult and become a child who also wants to believe in the unbelievable.

And once Joanne becomes that child, almost anything can and does happen.

From the opening passages of *Harry Potter and the Sorcerer's Stone*, we can sense that something quite out of the ordinary is up. Our introduction to Harry is not a happy one. He is an orphan who has been living for ten years in a closet under the stairs of his cruel aunt and uncle's house. But we soon discover that Harry is not an ordinary soul. He is the son of wizards. However, Harry does not have a clue that he even has these powers until one day a giant appears out of nowhere and delivers to Harry a scholarship to the Hogwarts School of Witchcraft and Wizardry.

Once there, Harry discovers friends, foes, his magical powers, and a mission to get rid of the evil that lies hidden in the depths of the school. In the classic sense, friends unite, evil is banished, at least temporarily, and all is well.

There is much more of the same in *Harry Potter and the Chamber of Secrets,* as a more mature Harry and his friends once again battle evil while the young wizard begins to learn more about his adopted land. And what he finds, thanks to Joanne's vivid imagination, is surprises around every corner. There is the diary that writes back, a dead professor who continues to teach class, and portraits of long-dead ancestors who come alive at night to primp and curl their hair.

By the third book, *Harry Potter and the Prisoners of Azkaban*, the author has seen fit to darken things up. In the Dementors, we see truly disgusting evil. But Harry has by this time grown wise enough and powerful enough to fight the good fight. There is also that priceless moment when Harry discovers Cho Chan on the Quidditch field and thinks to himself that she is kind of pretty.

Joanne has filled the page with enticing images and has us hooked.

"I really can, with no difficulty at all, think myself back to eleven years old," said Rowling in a *Time* magazine interview of her ability to tap into her own childhood when writing. "I can remember being a kid and being very powerless and having this whole underworld that to adults is always going to be impenetrable. I think that I have very vivid memories of how it felt to be Harry's age."

On more than one occasion, Joanne has acknowledged her childhood memories as an influence. For her, Hermione is very much herself as a child. And while there was no real-life Harry in her life, she has said that many elements of the character have come from people she knew. And her enemies? They spring to life when Joanne remembers the times when she had to face the school bully and did not know whether she would come out okay.

The author has said that what she likes about writing the adventures of Harry Potter, and what brings her willingly to the task every day, is the notion of opening up a world of dreams and its possibilities.

"When you dream, you can do what you like," she has told *Newsweek.*

And there have been dreams aplenty in the first three Harry Potter adventures, *Harry Potter and the Philosopher's Stone* (retitled *Harry Potter and the Sorcerer's Stone* in America), *Harry Potter and the Chamber of Secrets*, and *Harry Potter and the Prisoner of Azkaban.* The world Harry Potter inhabits is dotted with strange creatures like Buckbeak, Scabbers, and Crookshanks. There are good people like Professor Dumbledore and Hagrid and bad people like the Dursleys and the evil Lord

Voldemort. In the world of Harry Potter, owls run banks, apprentice students chase after balls on flying broomsticks, and apprentice wizards tread lightly as they enter the Forbidden Forest.

But finally it is Harry Potter, a skinny thirteen-year-old with glasses, green eyes, and a head of unruly black hair who is the heart and soul of J. K. Rowling's adventures. The author feels that Harry is a mirror into her young readers' souls.

"Harry is smart and good at sports and a lot of things that other children would like to be," Rowling once told an interviewer. "But children also feel for him because he has lost his parents. If an author makes a character an orphan, few children will want to be an orphan too. But it is a freeing thing because a certain weight of parental expectation is lifted."

Yet the adventures of Harry Potter are much more than merely escape for the preteen set. Adults have also taken Harry to their hearts and marvel at the simplicity and positive values presented in the tales. Harry often is the center of a family's time together. Parents read to their children and children often read out loud to their parents. Or parents, after their children have gone to sleep, have been known to sit down with the book and read it themselves.

The author regularly reads her fan mail and so is well aware that the power of Harry Potter to capture readers has spanned the generations. A woman from Glasgow, Scotland, recently wrote to Joanne's British publisher asking how to go about joining the Harry Potter Fan Club, adding as an aside that she was sixty years old. An Englishman, when inquiring about the possibility of a Harry Potter movie, described himself as "a child at heart, an adult in body." She has had reports of family squabbles breaking out at bedtime when a parent wanted to finish reading a chapter and ended up taking the book from her children so she could read the book herself.

Joanne has thought long and hard about why people of all ages respond to Harry, and she thinks she knows the reason why.

"I think some of the reason is that Harry has to accept adult burdens in his life, although he is a child," she said in a recent interview. "There's something very endearing about that to kids and adults as well. Harry is also an old-fashioned hero. There's enough human frailty in Harry that people of all ages can identify with."

The author also points to a sense of morality that runs through each book. Rather than preach, she gets her messages across quite naturally and humanly in the actions and thoughts of her characters. As we have discovered in the first four books, Harry Potter is not the perfect little boy. He bends and breaks the rules when it suits his purpose and has all the insecurities of a normal boy or girl. Children and adults tend to love the fact that they can open a Harry Potter book and see themselves in the characters.

Arthur Levine, the U.S. editor of the Harry Potter books, feels that a big attraction to readers is the idea of growing up underappreciated, feeling like an outcast, and then suddenly bursting forth into the light and being discovered. "That is the fantasy of every person who grows up smart but not very athletic. That's the emotional connection that drew me to the books," he told *The New York Times.*

Whatever the reason, Harry Potter has become

a worldwide phenomenon since the publication of the first book in 1997. To date, the first four books have sold more than 10 million copies in over a hundred different languages. The books continue to reside at or near the top of a number of best-seller lists, and a movie studio is in the process of making a big-budget movie of *Harry Potter and the Sorcerer's Stone* that will be in movie theaters all over when this edition of the book is out!

But there is more to the popularity of Harry Potter than book sales and movie deals. Kids have taken Harry to their hearts, and he has become a very real part of their playtime. They have made up games and put on plays centered around Harry and his adventures. Many of the numerous computer Web sites that have sprung up around the Harry Potter books feature original stories written by fans. Groups of children gather regularly to read Harry Potter out loud. One enterprising eleven-year-old even had "Educated at Hogwarts" printed up on business cards so he could hand them out to his friends.

Surprisingly, the author behind the fantastic adventures of Harry Potter is a person of relatively simple pleasures and tastes. She told an Internet site that she has no hobbies "except hanging out with my friends and writing." Her favorite holiday is Halloween. Her favorite television shows are British comedies and the U.S. imports *Frasier* and *The Simpsons.*

"I get bored with my life," she once said. "I prefer inventing things."

But for Rowling, the true joy comes in the stories of how young children have embraced her tales. And they certainly have. A family in California was so anxious to read *Harry Potter and the Prisoner of Azkaban* that they went on the Internet and ordered a British copy of the book so that they would not have to wait months for the book to be published in America. When her third book went on sale at 3:45 P.M., the precise moment when English schools let out for the day, she was amazed when stores sold out every copy in a matter of minutes.

Rowling, who is often shy about doing interviews and has proven very secretive when asked about the further adventures of Harry, came to enjoy book tours. In fact, she gets a lot of pleasure from book signings, when she gets to meet her young audience face-to-face. One example of this occurred during a visit to a school in England when she was approached by a young boy carrying one of her books. "He recited the first page of the first book to me from memory," she explained to *Newsweek*. "When he stopped, he said, 'I can go on.' He continued reciting the first five pages of the book. That was unbelievable."

However, she said, during a *Scholastic* online chat, one of her most gratifying moments came about during a reading and book signing appearance in her hometown of Edinburgh. "The event was sold out and the queue for signing at the end was very long. When a twelve-year-old girl finally reached me, she said, 'I didn't want there to be so many people here, because this is my book!' I told her that was exactly how I feel about my favorite books. Nobody else has a right to know them, let alone like them!"

What can best be described as Pottermania occurred last year when Joanne came to the United States on yet another book tour. Her many stops at bookstores across the country continued to amaze her and showed the author that while Harry Potter books are written in a distinctly British style, the messages of her books are international.

During a reading in a high school gymnasium in Santa Rosa, California, Joanne was shocked when she looked out and saw 2,500 Harry Potter fans jumping up and down on the bleachers and shouting "Harry! Harry!" at the top of their lungs.

The scene repeated itself in San Francisco, California, when Joanne's car rounded a corner and the writer was amazed to find more than a thousand people standing in line in front of a bookstore for a 9:30 A.M. reading and autograph session. She would later discover that many of the children and their parents had spent the night in line just so they could make sure they would get in for the event. One family had even made the six-hour trip by car from Los Angeles the night before just so they could be first in line. Joanne gave a short reading, answered her fan's many questions, and then signed a thousand books in two hours. And then, quick as a flash, she was back inside her limo and gone.

"It was a little like having the Beatles here,"

said an excited, out-of-breath bookstore representative to *Entertainment Weekly* after the event. "Kids will probably be coming here for years saying 'Wow! That's where the Harry Potter lady was standing.' "

For J. K. Rowling, the success of Harry Potter has been a fantasy all its own. After years of struggles in unfulfilling jobs, living in poverty, and trying to make a go of it as a single mother, the author now lives comfortably in Scotland and regularly travels around the world. She has often reflected on how her reaction to the success of Harry "has been shock" and that "it was like being catapulted into fairyland."

"I always find it difficult to be objective about Harry," she once admitted to BBC Online when discussing the question of reality and fantasy in her books. "To me, they remain my own private little world. For five years, they were my own private secret. From the moment I had the idea for the book, I could see a lot of comic potential in the idea that wizards walk among us."

But finally J. K. Rowling's success is a dream come true. "I would have been crazy to have expected what has happened to Harry," she has said. "The mere fact of being able to say I was a published author was the fulfillment of a dream I've had since I was a very young child."

2

RABBIT AND
MISS BEE

J. K. Rowling's parents met on a train in 1963. And as in all good fairy tales, it was love at first sight.

At first look Peter Rowling and his bride-to-be could not have been more different. Peter was the manager of an aircraft factory, while Ann worked as a lab technician. He came from a blue-collar world, while she was into books and more intellectual pursuits. However, none of those differences seemed to matter.

Because as they courted, fell in love, and eventually decided to get married, they discovered that they did indeed have a lot in common. They shared a good sense of humor, and both believed in the importance of home and family life. They also loved the English countryside and good books. When they walked down the aisle, Peter and Ann felt that they had each found the perfect mate.

Shortly after their marriage, Peter and Ann moved into a small but comfortable home in the tiny hamlet of Chipping Sodbury. The couple loved the idea of living literally in the middle of England's famed forests and hillsides. But they had always been city dwellers, so they enjoyed their regular trips into the nearby town of Bristol, where they would shop and idle away the hours together.

Peter and Ann felt they had the perfect life. Only one thing could enrich their story.

And that came in November 1965, when the couple announced to family and friends that Ann was pregnant with their first child. The next nine months were a joyous and exciting time for Peter and Ann as they made preparations for the arrival of their child. They speculated about whether their child would be a boy or a girl and discussed names for the child at great length. They regularly wandered into the room that had been picked out as the baby's room and planned where the crib would be and what colors the walls should be painted.

As is true of all parents, they hoped that the child would be healthy and happy. Late in July 1966, Peter's car pulled up in front of Chipping Sodbury General Hospital. It was time.

Joanne Kathleen Rowling came kicking and screaming into the world on July 31, 1966. In later years, Joanne would look back on the occasion of her birth as an omen of things to come. "I think it is rather appropriate for someone who collects funny names to be born in a hospital named Chipping Sodbury," she laughed in an online biography.

Almost from the moment Joanne was born, Peter and Ann sensed the bright, inquisitive nature of their child. Her eyes were always wide in amazement at the world around her, and she was always grasping and touching things with curiosity. They could almost predict that one of the first words out of their daughter's mouth would be *why*.

Joanne once described her early childhood years as "dreamy." The young child seemed to have a knack for solitary pursuits. She often played imaginary games in her room or in the tall grass in her backyard. If there was a tree around, she would climb it. If other children approached her, Joanne was quick to invite them to join her in any number of games. Even in those early years, she was very fond of the idea of "let's pretend."

Hoping to nurture their child's imagination, Joanne's parents began reading to her at an early age. Because both parents were constant readers, it is no surprise that one of the author's earliest memories was of "the house being full of books and of my parents constantly reading to me." Joanne was fed a steady diet of fairy tales and fantasy books as well as a smattering of the classics.

Even during her most uncomfortable moments, the sounds of her parents reading to her always had a calming effect.

"My most vivid memory of childhood is my father sitting and reading *The Wind in the Willows* to me," she told the London *Daily Telegraph*. "I had the measles at the time, but I don't really remember that. I just remember the book."

What her parents did not realize was that a constant exposure to literature—in particular, to fairy tales and stories of the fantastic—had made an enormous impression on the young child. She began to dream up fantastic, well-plotted stories with larger-than-life characters. When she was at play, her stories were full of character and detail light-years beyond those generally produced by a child of her age.

Although she was too young to think in terms of what she wanted to be when she grew up, Joanne Kathleen Rowling, at a very early age, had this image of herself as somebody who would put pencil to paper and create magic worlds. "Writing for me has always been a kind of wonderful compulsion," she said in a 1999 interview of her early inclination to write. "I don't think anyone could have made me do it or could have prevented me from doing it. It's weird, but writing is all I ever wanted to do."

But these were private thoughts for Joanne, that wonderful secret that kept her warm and cozy in her bed at night and helped her to glide through her days. To tell even her parents would have ended all the fun.

But when her younger sister, Di, born less than two years after Joanne, reached age three, five-year-old Joanne "was big enough to hold her" sister down, so she began making up tall tales about fantastic creatures and imaginary places and telling them to Di.

These stories would often center on rabbits because, as Joanne has recalled, "we badly wanted a rabbit." One of the most memorable of these early flights of fantasy, and the one that always had Di roaring with little-girl laughter and excitement, was a story about how Di had fallen down a rabbit hole one day and ended up being fed strawberries by the rabbit family.

More often than not Di would sit fascinated by

her older sister's tales. She would inevitably ask Joanne to tell her the same story again and again, and because the stories were not written down, they would often come out slightly different in the retelling. Joanne was encouraged by her younger sister's response to begin jotting her stories down on paper. So one day, not long after she turned six, Joanne sat down with pencil and paper and wrote her first story.

Not surprisingly, it was a story about a rabbit called Rabbit. Out of this child came a fanciful tale of a rabbit who got the measles and was visited by a number of friends, including a giant bee named Miss Bee. "I wrote stories about rabbits for a couple of years. I definitely had a rabbit fixation," she once told an interviewer.

Di was thrilled with the story. Joanne's parents, who had taken to eavesdropping on their daughter's fantasy games, were amused by their daughter's imagination but did not feel it necessary to encourage her in any way. But their encouragement was not really necessary, because Joanne had already made up her mind that she was going to be a writer. "Ever since Rabbit and

Miss Bee, I knew I wanted to be a writer," she told *School Library Journal*. "I cannot overstate how much I wanted that. But I would rarely tell anyone so. I just never really spoke about it because I was embarrassed. And because my parents were the kind of parents who would have thought 'Ah yes, that's very nice, dear. But where is the pension plan?' "

Joanne grew into a bright child whose imagination was often the talk of the neighborhood. This talent was also a topic during her first years in school, when her teachers would marvel at the maturity and creativity of her early reports and papers. Joanne took these early compliments as a sign that she had found something she was good at.

Another one of the young girl's early attempts at storytelling was a story of chills and adventure called *The Seven Cursed Diamonds*. "At that age I thought it was a novel," she would recall in later years. "But I think now that it was only a very long short story."

Joanne was doing more than writing during those early years. It was the rare moment when her parents did not find her nose buried in a book. The young child was quite outgoing and had a number of friends in the neighborhood but always seemed to prefer to go off by herself and read. Among her favorites was *The Little White Horse* by Elizabeth Goudge, *Manxmouse* by Paul Gallico, and the Narnia books by C. S. Lewis.

"I adored E. Nesbit," she once said of her reading habits. "I think her books are wonderful. I also liked Noel Streatfeild, who did those girly books about ballet shoes and things. Even now, if I was in a room with one of the Narnia books, I would pick it up and re-read it like a shot," she explained to the London *Telegraph*.

Shortly after Joanne began to write, her parents decided that they needed a bigger home and moved the family to the small town of Yate, just outside of Bristol. Less than a year after they moved to Yate, Peter and Ann decided that they liked the scenery better on the other side of Bristol and moved the family to yet another small town, Winterbourne.

Joanne and Di adjusted to the moves just fine

and were quick to make friends with the neighborhood children. Winterbourne, in particular, had a lot of children Joanne and Di's age; they were immediately welcomed into the informal gang that would play games up and down the streets of the town. In those days, Joanne was very much a tomboy, engaging in just about every rough-and-tumble game without worrying about falling down and hurting herself. Even at that age, Joanne was not what you would call athletic and would often fall. But her persistence in trying soon gained her the respect of the neighborhood children.

Two of her closest friends in Winterbourne were a brother and sister named Ian and Vikki Potter. In later years, Ian Potter would tell *Book* magazine that when his sister and he would get together with Joanne and her sister, they would occasionally tell stories. "But most of all we liked dressing up, and nine times out of ten, it would be Joanne who would say, 'Oh, let's play witches and wizards.' "

Joanne remembered being quite close to Ian

and Vikki during their days in Winterbourne. One reason for their friendship was their name.

"Their surname was Potter," she once recalled. "I always liked the name."

3

CHILDISH THINGS

S hortly after Joanne Kathleen Rowling turned nine, her parents decided it was time to move once again. Only this time it was because her parents' dream had finally come true.

Peter and Ann Rowling had both been born and raised in London and were basically city folk at heart. But because it was cheaper to live in the country, they had postponed any notion of living in a city. However, as Peter moved up in his job as a mechanic for an automobile factory and began receiving a higher salary, the couple decided it was time to make the move.

The couple, despite their yearning for city life, had grown to like the presence of forests and hillsides in their life. Rather than a big city, the Rowlings decided small would be better.

Tutshill is a small village situated near Chepstow in the Forest of Dean. It was very much a city with streets, stores, and schools. But the river Wye ran by and there were fields all around, making it the ideal mixture of city and country.

Joanne and Di quickly adjusted to their new surroundings. They would frolic for hours by the river and make up fantasy games to carry out in the fields. Joanne was outgoing and soon made friends in her neighborhood. When she felt comfortable enough, she would bring out some of her stories and read them to the neighborhood kids. While the other children did not quite know what to make of this little girl who used big words and told funny stories about fantastic places, they were impressed and gladly made room for a regular storytime from Joanne.

She would continue to enjoy playground activities, but reading and writing, which are solitary pursuits, remained first on her list of passions.

When it came to books, she was already reading well beyond her grade level. At age nine, Joanne discovered Ian Fleming's James Bond novels, and they became a regular part of her reading pastime.

Not too long after that she discovered the works of Jane Austen and was never the same again. Austen's delicate passages and detailed stories became a model for Joanne Rowling. "Jane Austen is my favorite author, ever."

There was only one drawback to living in the town of Tutshill. Joanne had to go to Tutshill Primary School. And Joanne hated her new school.

"It was a very small, very old-fashioned place," she painfully remembered for the Okubooks Web site. "The rolltop desks still had inkwells."

But that was not the only problem Joanne had with the school. There was her new teacher, Mrs. Morgan, to deal with. And Mrs. Morgan scared the life out of Joanne. Mrs. Morgan was a strict, no-nonsense type of teacher who taught her class according to the book. Unfortunately for Joanne, Mrs. Morgan's book and her new student did not agree when it came to mathematics.

"She gave me an arithmetic test on the very first morning, and, after a huge effort, I managed to get zero right out of ten," she said on an Oku-books chat. "The test was on fractions and I had never done fractions before."

On her first day, Mrs. Morgan sat Joanne in a row of desks to the far right of the classroom. The young child was fine with that until a few days later when she figured out, by talking to her fellow students, that the teacher had put her in the stupid row.

It seemed that Mrs. Morgan had made up her seating chart based on how clever she thought her students were. The brightest students sat on the left side of the room and the rest sat on the right. Joanne painfully recalled her first days at Tutshill Primary, when, she wrote, "I was as far right as I could get without sitting on the playground."

It was a tough first year for Joanne. She was not making friends as easily as she had in the past.

Physically and emotionally she was changing. It all added up to a rough beginning in her new school.

"I wasn't as clever as I thought I should be," she confessed when looking back on those days for *Salon* magazine. "I don't think I was a know-it-all. I was obsessed with achieving academically, but that masked a huge insecurity. I think it is very common for plain young girls to feel this way. I definitely would not want to go back and do childhood again. I don't look back on it as a phase of blissful happiness at all."

She was the new kid in school, and she had to deal with the embarrassment of being identified as dumb. But Joanne managed to turn the experience around.

She studied hard and managed to make a small but loyal circle of friends. Not surprisingly, English was her best subject. Although she continued to write fantasy fables in her spare moments, she was not comfortable with sharing them with anybody but Di and one or two of her closest friends.

Joanne was determined to prove her teacher's impression of her wrong; by the end of the year, she had convinced Mrs. Morgan that she was not a dim bulb. One day she was rewarded when her teacher told her she could now sit on the left side of the classroom. Joanne recalled the promotion with mixed emotions.

"I had been promoted to second left. But the promotion was at a cost. Mrs. Morgan made me swap seats with my best friend. So in one short walk across the room, I became clever but unpopular," she said in her Web site entry.

Joanne regained her popularity and continued through her primary school years in an uneventful way. Her grades continued to be good. She remained painfully shy, with only a small circle of close friends. Writing continued to be her passion.

No matter how busy her days were, she always managed to find some quiet time to release her fantasies. Her stories, full of magic and funny characters with even funnier names, were the highlight of her sister's playtime. The praise Joanne received from Di and her parents convinced Joanne, even as young as she was, that she would one day be an important writer and would live a wonderful, fairy-tale life.

Joanne successfully graduated from Tutshill Primary and was soon on her way to Wyedean Comprehensive School for middle school. The confidence and positive self-image that Joanne had fought hard to cultivate during elementary school disappeared during her first year at Wyedean Comprehensive.

She became insecure at the prospect of attending school with older children. Plus she was going through puberty and thus felt very insecure. It also did not help that she wore glasses. "I was quiet, freckly, short-sighted, and rubbish at sports," she once said.

But Joanne managed to find her niche at Wyedean. Eventually she found other girls like her—quiet, smart, and not quite popular—and she became a part of that group. She did quite well in school, with English and foreign languages being her favorite subjects.

The youngster slowly began to come out of her shell at Wyedean. She was continuing to write and finally felt confident enough to risk it all by reading some of her stories to her new friends. They liked what they heard and were regularly entertained by Joanne's creative efforts.

"I used to tell my equally quiet and studious friends long serial stories during lunchtime," she wrote in an essay. "They usually involved us all doing heroic and daring deeds we certainly would not have done in real life."

Joanne breezed through her comprehensive school years on a steady course with relatively few noteworthy achievements. There was the embarrassment of breaking her arm one day while playing the very noncontact sport of net ball. There was also the day Joanne became the big girl on campus when she was attacked by the toughest girl in her grade. She would later recall that she would logically have preferred to run from trouble rather than stand and fight. But fight back is exactly what she ended up doing.

"I didn't have a choice," she once said. "It was hit back or lie down and play dead. For a few days I was quite famous because she hadn't managed to flatten me. The truth was, my locker was right behind me and it held me up."

Unfortunately, Joanne's newfound reputation

as a tough girl lasted only a short time. She soon reverted to timidity and would spend weeks peering nervously around corners, in constant fear of being ambushed.

Through her later years in comprehensive school, Joanne began to come out of her shell. Her confidence growing, she was now quicker to speak up in class and was more assertive in nonschool conversations and activities. While still what would be considered very unathletic, she was now more inclined to mix it up with the other girls. This, she would later report, was due in part to the fact that her glasses had been replaced by contact lenses, so she was less fearful of getting hit in the face.

In fact, Joanne, by her own reports, flowered in her teen years. She felt that, personally and socially, things had actually begun to get better and she finally came to the all-important realization that there was more to Joanne Kathleen Rowling than someone who was driven to get everything right. Joanne was suddenly very comfortable with herself.

Like most normal teenagers, Joanne had a growing sense of independence; this would lead to the occasional row with her parents, usually short-lived arguments over very little. Her relationship with Di remained close. When not helping her younger sibling with her homework, Joanne would continue to use Di as her first audience for the many stories she was continuing to write. The second group to hear her latest tales was her girlfriends at school.

Despite the fact that she had numerous teachers who saw something in her and encouraged her in a creative direction, writing remained a largely private pursuit. The stories she felt confident enough to share were often the tales of action and adventure that featured herself and her friends as thinly disguised characters in stories of derring-do.

Her other stories, those she perceived as more intimate, she would not show to anyone. These were the stories that she felt a real writer would write. And she was not quite ready to let the outside world into that part of her creative life.

Joanne's love for reading continued to blossom as well. She had long since begun to read about the lives of real people and had developed a particular infatuation for author Jessica Mitford, a feminist who ran off and joined the Spanish Civil War at age nineteen and was a passionate supporter of human rights. "I remember reading the book *Hons and Rebels* at age fourteen, and it changed my life."

Joanne had grown into quite the confident student in her senior year at Wyedean Comprehensive. She was popular and outgoing, and her grades were quite good. So good, in fact, that Joanne was made Head Girl in her final year.

Head Girl was a lofty position that all the girls aspired to. But, in fact, very little responsibility was attached to the title. Once a year, when some noblewoman from the region came to visit the school, it was the job of the Head Girl to show her around the school fair. The requirement that Joanne dreaded the most was that the Head Girl also had to give a talk to the whole school.

"I decided to play them a record to cut down on the time that I had to speak to them," she laughingly recalled in a Web site memory. "Well, the record was scratched, and right in the middle of playing, it began skipping and played the same line over and over again. Finally the deputy head-mistress came out on stage and kicked it."

Joanne ended her years at Wyedean Compre-hensive with high honors. Her teachers were pre-dicting a bright future for her. Her parents were proud. Joanne Kathleen Rowling was quiet on the subject of her future. She knew in her heart of hearts what she wanted to do with her life. She had her own hopes and dreams.

Now all she had to do was figure out how to make them come true.

4

LIFE LESSONS

J oanne wanted to write. But being admittedly "the most disorganized person in the whole world," she did not know how to begin. So she would write something, read through it, and usually find enough fault in her work to discard it. Even when she was happy with a story, it still remained her own private happiness.

She had boxes and folders full of short stories, but did not have a clue how one went about getting them published. She knew magazines bought such stories all the time but never saw fit to submit one. Plus, even thinking about doing so usually ended up with Joanne backing down in the face of her old fears of letting other people judge her work.

So, like so many others, Joanne was an eighteen-year-old with definite ideas but lacking the courage to carry them out. This was a side of herself that Joanne did not particularly like, and she would often upbraid herself for being too cowardly to extend herself. But the truth was that Joanne Kathleen Rowling was just not ready to take on the world.

Because Joanne was frustrated at her inability to take that next big step in her writing life, she was easily influenced by others. Consequently, she was willing to take her parent's advice.

Peter and Ann, having not been privy to her writing ambitions, had long been bewildered at their eldest daughter's seeming lack of direction. Joanne's parents had regularly suggested that with her love of language, their daughter should study French and literature, which would lead to a wonderful career as a bilingual legal secretary. And with her good grades, they felt Exeter University would be the ideal place for her to go.

Joanne's heart was in her writing and she felt that pursuing any other line of work would be a mistake. However, being an obedient child, Joanne reluctantly took her parents' advice and was soon enrolled at Exeter.

The teenager was encouraged by the stories she had heard that Exeter was a liberal school that was big on unconventional ideas. She figured that, if nothing else, she would find much to influence her in her true passions. In fact, what she discovered shortly after enrolling was that Exeter was actually a conservative school wrapped up in traditional ideals. "It was fantastic," she told a reporter, "but it did not offer quite the chance to be a radical that I planned."

Joanne's years at Exeter were productive. She found that she was able to master French fairly easily. A big part of her education at Exeter was a year spent in Paris, learning to use the French language in a practical setting. Joanne found the year abroad exhilarating.

She took in the sights and marveled at being in

another country for the first time without her family. Joanne grew up during that year in Paris. By the time she returned to Exeter, Joanne Kathleen Rowling had grown confident in her ability to make her way in the world.

During this time Joanne had her first serious relationship. Being in love and having someone care about her was an important thing for her. Joanne reveled in the fact that she was, in fact, attractive enough and bright enough to gain the affections of a terrific boy.

Of course every spare moment was taken up with writing. There was the usual batch of short stories that only a handful of people ever saw. She also attempted a novel. But while she was confident in other areas, Joanne steadfastly refused to submit any of her stories, belittling them any time anyone would suggest that her stories were good and that she should send them out.

This lack of confidence in the thing she valued most haunted her every waking hour. In her heart, Joanne knew that it was time to shake off the bonds. Unfortunately her head still had a firm hold on her fears and insecurities. So she continued to do nothing at all.

Joanne graduated from Exeter with honors, and as often happens, she and her boyfriend naturally drifted apart. But Joanne had little time to grieve over a lost love. She was soon going out on her first job interviews.

Getting dressed up and presenting herself at job interviews was not something the young woman liked doing. It seemed like a silly, unnecessary game. It made her feel totally inadequate and very much like a little girl again. Besides, this was not what she really wanted to do, which was to write fabulous stories, see them published, and be able to keep writing, and live happily ever after. But since she was not willing to take the risks necessary to reach that pinnacle, Joanne would have to contend with the real world.

The next six years were a rough introduction to the often tedious life of the workaday world. Joanne went through a series of jobs. In one instance, she spent two years researching human rights violations for Amnesty International. While she felt she was doing important work and that her idol, Jessica Mitford, would approve, the work itself soon became predictable and boring, two things Joanne could not abide.

For the most part, she held a seemingly endless string of boring secretarial jobs. The work did not interest her and she was not making a lot of money. Plus, as she has readily admitted, "I later proved to be the worst secretary ever."

Her mind always seemed to be on something else. "Whatever job I had, I was always writing like crazy," she once wrote. "All I ever liked about offices was being able to type up stories on the computer when no one was looking. I was never paying much attention in meetings because I was usually scribbling bits of my latest stories in the margins of the pad or thinking up names for my characters. This is a problem when you're supposed to be taking the minutes of the meeting."

Needless to say, Joanne's employers frowned on her writing fantasy stories on company time, and she was dismissed from a couple of her jobs. But for the most part, Joanne simply got tired of doing work she detested and would eventually quit. Well into her twenties, the young woman was like a boat without a rudder.

Joanne's parents were supportive but concerned that their older daughter seemed to be having trouble finding her place in life. Her only solace in an otherwise bleak world was her writing.

"I was writing a lot of short stories and a lot of started and abandoned novels," she told *School Library Journal* of that period in her life. "I felt I worked very hard and had served my apprenticeship in terms of writing." She felt less than positive about herself when those works would inevitably end up in a box with all the other stories that had not seen the light of day.

Unfortunately, all the hard work still did not add up to much, so Joanne reluctantly searched for yet another job. This time she found employment as an office worker for the Manchester Chamber of Commerce.

Joanne had another reason for going to Manchester. She had received a letter from her old boyfriend at Exeter, stating that he was in Manchester and that he'd like to see her again. The job she got was as dull and boring to her as all the others had been, but this time she was determined to make a go of things.

Joanne made time for her old boyfriend but remained diligent in her writing. At lunchtime, she would make her way to one of the nearby pubs or cafés, settle at an out-of-the-way table, and write. While far from antisocial, she would often find herself praying that nobody in the office was having a birthday or some other celebration that would require her to join in, taking up her precious writing time.

Joanne looked upon the commute between her London home and Manchester as her private time. She would often while away the time reading a book, working on her latest story, or simply staring out the window at the passing scenery. One day, as she returned to London after yet another day of unrewarding work, the train suddenly ground to a halt.

There was some kind of mechanical problem that, it was announced, would require a delay of about four hours. Normally this would have been ideal. But since Joanne was too tired to either read or write, she focused her attention on a group of cows, grazing in a meadow in front of her.

What she did not realize was that her life was about to change. "I was sitting on the train, just staring out the window at some cows. It was not the most inspiring subject. When all of a sudden the idea for Harry just appeared in my mind's eye. I can't tell you why or what triggered it. But I saw the idea of Harry and the wizard school very plainly. I suddenly had this basic idea of a boy who didn't know what he was," she said in a *School Library Journal* conversation.

Joanne was enthralled with the vision that had come to her. She immediately reached for a pen and paper to begin jotting down notes and thoughts. Unfortunately, Joanne had neither. And so, with nothing but her memory to serve her, she sat quietly and just played with the notion of characters, funny names, and story possibilities.

By the time her train stopped at Knight's Cross station in London, Joanne had the basic premise of the first Harry Potter story down. Over the next few weeks and months, Joanne put every free moment into jotting down ideas and stories centered around this imaginary boy and his adventures in a world ruled by magic. The Harry Potter files soon filled one box, then several.

Joanne continued her job at the Manchester Chamber of Commerce but took every opportunity before, during, and after work to fashion a single story line for the first Harry Potter book. In short order she came up with Harry, an orphan being raised by a cruel aunt and uncle, who after finding out he is a young wizard is whisked off to a boarding school for young wizards called Hogwarts.

Joanne would often find herself smiling as she created bits of adventure for Harry and unusual names for the characters that would populate his world. Her whole outlook improved once she was inspired by Harry. Her parents and sister noticed the change, but they knew little about what had caused it. Joanne dropped little hints about something she was working on but stopped short of revealing all. She felt that to let too much out would blunt the magic.

Joanne Kathleen Rowling was already thinking like a resident of Harry Potter's world.

But this period of good spirits would be short-lived. Her mother, who had been diagnosed with multiple sclerosis in the past year, died suddenly at the age of forty-five.

Joanne was distraught. She was well aware that her mother was ill but had no idea that MS would take her so quickly, and she felt terribly guilty that she had not been there in her mother's final hours. Her deepest regret was that she had never let her mother read any of Harry.

In her distracted state of mind, the young girl had a tough time concentrating on work, so not too long after that, Joanne lost her job at the Manchester Chamber of Commerce.

"It was a nightmare period," sighed Joanne. She told *People* Magazine that writing about Harry was the only thing that got her through.

William Mercer McCleod

William Mercer McCleod

5

HARRY IS BORN

Joanne was in an emotional whirlwind. She had just turned twenty-six. She was once again out of work. The relationship with her boyfriend once again seemed to be going nowhere. And she was in a constantly saddened state because of the death of her mother.

The only real joy in her life was Harry Potter.

She had continued to work diligently on the book, with boxes overflowing with ideas, names, and fragments of stories. Joanne was feeling confident in what she had jotted down and began seriously contemplating writing the novel. But she was torn between living out her dream of a life dedicated to writing and the guilt she was feeling at not being like everyone else.

Joanne was thinking very hard about what her life was about and what she wanted to do with it. One of the bright spots she kept coming back to was that year she spent in Paris working as an assistant teacher. She had enjoyed it and thought she might enjoy it again. In any case, she felt she needed to do something constructive with her life.

Joanne's dreams of teaching in some far-off land finally won out. In September 1990, she announced to her family and friends that she would no longer settle for menial office work and soon accepted the offer of a job abroad, teaching English as a second language at a school in the northern Portugal town of Oporto. Joanne was both excited and frightened at the prospect of going so far away to work, but she felt that being away from home and family was the only way she would ultimately find herself.

So she packed her bags, many of which contained her notes on Harry, kissed her father and sister goodbye and promised them she would write on a regular basis. Before she knew it, she was on her way.

Although she was homesick, Joanne quickly adjusted to life in Portugal. She immediately found a comfortable apartment to live in and became well acquainted with the country, its people, and its customs. She loved walking the quaint streets, window shopping, and dealing, often unsuccessfully with the Portuguese delicacy tripe (the fatty lining of animal stomach). The people were friendly and it was sunny and warm all the time, a real contrast to the gloomy, cold weather in London. After a short while the homesickness disappeared and Joanne settled into the life of a teacher.

Joanne's students took an immediate liking to her. And when they were not making fun of her name, calling her "Rolling Stone," they would sit in rapt attention as Joanne taught them the fine art of speaking English. The transplanted Londoner was happy with the progress her students were making and proud of the good notices she had been receiving from the school superiors. She was also happy that her schedule allowed her to continue to write. "I worked afternoons and evenings," she recalled, "and so I had my mornings free to write."

Harry and his adventures at wizard school were slowly but surely coming together. The first pages of the novel were written in a wave of excitement. Joanne was discovering Harry much in the manner that her creation was discovering his magic—in short bursts of enthusiasm that often had her breaking into a spontaneous grin as the words flowed from her mind to the page.

She would chuckle as the names Hermione, Ron, Hagrid, and Dumbledore instantly became immortalized in the forms of Harry's many fantastic friends. Naming her characters was one of the most enjoyable parts about writing Harry. Long a collector of unusual names and clever when it came to creating her own, Joanne would often laugh uncontrollably when the likes of an Every Flavor Beans or a Justin Finch Fletchey would spring spontaneously to mind.

"Having a child who escapes the confines of the

adult world and goes somewhere where he has power really appealed to me," the author once revealed to *The Boston Globe* of her feelings while writing the first Harry Potter book. "There's always room for a story that can transport readers to another place."

But the excitement was often tempered by the frustration of trying to get everything about Harry and his world just right. The author admitted to some tears in those early days when, in detailing Harry's life as an orphan, she was forced to deal with the passing of her own mother.

Evil was also a notion that Joanne had to deal with when creating the villainous Lord Voldemort. Rather than create bad guys typical of a children's book—noisy but not truly evil—she decided that evil in the world of Harry Potter would ring true to readers only if it was serious and its consequences fell on characters that the readers loved.

Ultimately the thing that caused Joanne the most concern was the tone of the books. From the beginning, Joanne was torn between writing the typical children's book, which often condescended to the reader, or simply writing the book that she would choose to read as an adult. Joanne chose the latter course.

Writing this book, despite the obstacles and challenges involved, was a constant joy—one that would help her through the occasional bouts of loneliness. Joanne was friendly and outgoing with her co-workers but had remained reserved and shy around men. Despite having a boyfriend at Exeter, she had never thought of herself as pretty and so had never been too concerned that the years were rolling by without the prospects of a husband or a family in her life.

But all of that changed the day Joanne Kathleen Rowling fell in love.

She and he had met by chance. He was a journalist for one of the leading television stations in Portugal. Joanne, blushing like a schoolgirl, had been instantly attracted to his bright smile and his dark good looks. As they began to date, Joanne also discovered that he was bright, sensitive, and interested in her.

Theirs was a whirlwind courtship. Within months

of their meeting, Joanne and the handsome man from Portugal were married.

The first two years of their marriage were good if somewhat hectic times for the couple. Her husband's work often kept him out till all hours, and with her schedule, they often found it difficult to find private time together. Still, Joanne found inspiration in her happiness, and it showed in her enthusiasm for her work and the continued progress of Harry Potter.

What had started out as a simple tale for young children was becoming more detailed. What was intended as a book for young people was beginning to take on layers of depth equally suited for adult readers. The characters were living and breathing in a very real way; although children, they were making choices and behaving much more maturely than most characters in children's stories. And so it did not bother Joanne when Harry's adventures in Hogwarts grew, with no end in sight.

In 1992, Joanne discovered she was pregnant. The young couple was thrilled and, privately, the mother-to-be hoped that the prospect of a baby in the house would help their relationship, which had hit a rough patch.

Sadly the pressures of married life, coupled with the hormonal changes in being pregnant, soon began to weigh on Joanne. In her mind, her husband was always at work and was not showing her the kindness she had first seen in this man. Joanne would often lapse into fits of depression. There were tears. Her husband did his best to comfort her, but to no avail. Unfortunately the birth of the couple's daughter, Jessica, in 1993 did little to save the crumbling marriage.

"I was very depressed," Joanne remembered painfully in a UK News interview. "And having a newborn child made it doubly difficult. I simply felt like a nonperson. I was very low and I felt I had to achieve something."

In a matter of weeks, Joanne and her husband divorced. She has been rather secretive about her marriage, refusing to reveal the name of her husband or the actual reason for the divorce. She would only allow that "I've made my mistakes in that area. Just because you've got a good brain doesn't mean you're any better than the next person at keeping your hormones under control."

Joanne was in a terrible funk. She felt there was no reason to stay in Portugal, where the memory of her failed marriage would continue to haunt her and her prospects for any kind of life as a recently divorced woman with a child were limited. She was prepared to return to London, although the idea of returning home as a divorced single mother was not something she was looking forward to doing.

Joanne remained quiet and withdrawn in those days following the divorce. She was there for her daughter in every possible way. But she cried at the drop of a hat. And the worst part of all was that she rarely worked on the book.

In the midst of this depression, she received a telephone call from her sister, who was now quite grown and living in Edinburgh, Scotland. Di suggested that she might want to move to Edinburgh so that she could be near family while she decided what she would do next. Joanne agreed, taking Jessica, her bags, and the by now three chapters of *Harry Potter and the Sorcerer's Stone*, and hopped a train to Edinburgh. The ride to Edinburgh was long and lonely. As the weather turned from bright sunshine to dark and dreary, Joanne noted that it reflected her mood perfectly.

Although she was happy to be near her sister, once she arrived in Edinburgh, Joanne once again fell into deep despair. "I had a tiny baby, no job, and I was in a strange place," she painfully reflected in *People*.

These were not the best of times to be a single woman with a child in England and neighboring Scotland. Just a month earlier, the British prime minister, John Major, had given a speech scolding single parents for being welfare-loving freeloaders. Joanne felt particularly offended by that speech. Yes, she was a single mother with a child. But she was also a college graduate with no shortage of skills. Certainly she would be able to pull her head above water.

But as she walked around Edinburgh with Jessica, Joanne often felt the hard stares of strangers. It was as if they knew.

A guardian angel named Sean stepped forward and loaned Joanne enough money to put a deposit down on what she once called "a grotty flat." With a roof over their heads, Joanne faced the dilemma of what to do. Her heart was into finishing the Harry Potter book. But her dream was now complicated by the tiny bundle of joy asleep in her crib.

"I was terrified that I just wouldn't be able to justify to myself continuing to write," she told *School Library Journal*. "I thought it would be selfish for my daughter if I could earn a better living doing something else. If writing wasn't helping to buy new shoes, then it just felt very self-indulgent. What I was praying for was to just make enough for me to continue to write."

Christmas was fast approaching and the festivities of the season only seemed to make Joanne feel worse. She had no money for presents for her daughter and the dear friends who had been there for her. Joanne felt coming to Edinburgh had been a hasty decision, so she made plans to return to London and attempt to find another job after the first of the year.

One rainy afternoon, as she was visiting with her sister, Joanne, on an impulse, began telling her sister the story of Harry Potter, much as she had the story of Rabbit years ago. Di was immediately caught by the story and insisted that her older sister show her what she had written.

"It's possible that if she had not laughed, I would have set the whole thing to one side," recalled Joanne in the *Daily Telegraph* of that fateful moment.

"But Di did laugh."

6

DARK AND LIGHT

Making her sister laugh was the first positive experience Joanne had had in a long time. Encouraged that she might be on the right track with her book, Joanne made what she hoped would be a smart choice.

Joanne knew she would have no trouble finding another teaching job. But to do that would mean there would be no time left for writing. Finally she decided that she would finish the book in a year and try to get it published.

Joanne knew in her mind that this was a step that, once taken, could not be taken back. She was deliberately setting herself up for a hard time. But she also realized that she had spent years sitting on the fence about her writing, to no avail. To take a chance now would not put her in any worse a predicament then she was already in.

"I thought 'What is the worst that could happen?' Every publishing company in Britain could turn me down. Big deal," she explained to the *Daily Telegraph*.

Thinking that gave the young mother strength. But she was not foolhardy in approaching this decision. Once she made her decision, "my back was up against the wall, I knew I could not afford the luxury of writer's block."

Any idea of working while she wrote went out the window when she discovered that although she was eligible to receive public assistance, she was not eligible for child care. Thus Joanne was forced into unemployment. The author would later recall that at that point she found herself in "an appalling poverty trap" from which it seemed almost impossible to emerge.

The whole process of filing for public assistance was humiliating and demoralizing. Once again she was getting those nasty looks from strangers who saw her as something to be despised.

"That was probably the lowest point in my life," she confessed to *The Boston Globe*. "My self-respect was on the floor. I didn't want Jessica to grow up this way, so she became my inspiration and writing about Harry became my safe haven."

Joanne soon discovered that many of her so-called friends were suddenly not there for her. They gave her strange looks and what conversations they had with her were strained and forced.

But the young woman was also grateful for her sister and the handful of friends who stuck with her when the attitude around town was that Joanne was nothing more than a freeloader. If she needed a few pounds to tide her over, they were there. But more important, on those days when the writing was not going well, Jessica was a handful, and she was feeling miserable, Joanne had people around who would just sit and listen as she poured her heart out.

Public assistance barely covered rent and food,

so Joanne was forced to go to great lengths to save money. There were nights when there was barely enough food for mother and child, so Joanne would go to bed hungry. She could not afford even a used typewriter, and of course, even the most outdated computer was out of the question. So she would gather up scraps of paper and any pencils she could find and write out the adventures of Harry Potter in longhand.

Another problem was where to write. Her housing benefit only covered the rent on a cold, depressing one-room flat. This was hardly the place to inspire fantasy thoughts, and it was certainly not where Joanne wanted Jessica to spend the early part of her life. The struggling writer and mother put on her thinking cap and soon formulated an ingenious way to write and make her baby happy at the same time.

Every day she would put Jessica in her baby carrier and walk her around town until the child fell asleep. She would then head for one of a number of local cafés, where for the price of a cup of espresso and a glass of water, she could sit and write for a couple of hours while her daughter slept. Years later, Joanne would marvel at how much she had gotten done in those short periods of time.

One of her regular stops was the Nicolson Café, whose co-owner, Dougal McBride, remembered how he would glance up from his work and, sure enough, there would be Joanne writing away at a corner table. "She was quite an odd sight," he remembered in *People*. "She would just push the pram with one hand and write away."

Occasionally Joanne would be too tired or the weather would be too bleak for her to risk taking Jessica out and about, so she would be forced to write in the flat. These were the times when Joanne would think that things could not get any worse.

However, through all the tough times, Joanne was buoyed up by the good cheer she was finding in writing her novel. As the pages continued to pile up, Harry Potter became her imaginary white knight, righting all the wrongs in her fantasy world that could not be fixed in her own. Her eyes would grow intense and her mouth would grow tight when she was creating the latest diabolical deed for Voldemort. And then there was wise old Dumbledore, whose every appearance in her manuscript was a time for inner joy and celebration.

"I wasn't really aware that it was a children's book," she recalled in *Newsweek* of her feelings while writing *Harry Potter and the Sorcerer's Stone*. "I really wrote it for me. It was what I found funny and what I liked."

As she had hoped, writing *Harry Potter and the Sorcerer's Stone* was mentally and emotionally seeing her through the tough times. But as she got closer to completing the book, some of her old insecurities came flooding back. To fulfill her dream of becoming a writer, Joanne would have to risk all by sending the book out to publishers, who could dash her hopes without batting an eye.

Once she decided this was a risk worth taking, Joanne's next step was to figure out just how one went about getting published. She had heard stories about how one needed an agent in order to get one's work accepted by a book publisher. Now all she needed to do was find an agent.

Her first stop was the local library, where she found a writer's directory that listed the names and addresses of agents. Joanne pored over the directory and compiled a list of the agents she felt might be the most receptive to her book.

Harry Potter and the Sorcerer's Stone was completed early in 1994. Joanne went over the manuscript carefully, rewriting and polishing until she finally had the book exactly the way she had hoped. Because the cost of photocopying what had turned out to be an 80,000-word book was so prohibitive, Joanne, with the aid of a cheap typewriter she had managed to purchase, typed up two copies of her novel.

Then she sent the two copies to the top two agents on her list and hoped for the best.

The year 1994 became a turning point in Joanne's life. She had applied for and had received a grant from the Scottish Arts Council. The money was enough to allow Joanne to get proper child care for Jessica during the day. Encouraged by this, she began looking for work and soon found a job in Edinburgh as a teacher of French at the Leth Academy and, later, at the Moray House Training College. True to her word, a year to the day that

Joanne pulled into Edinburgh, penniless, she was now self-sufficient and off welfare.

Joanne Rowling was feeling reborn.

In her spare time, Joanne continued to play around with Harry Potter and had soon come up with a story line for a second book. She was hoping against hope that a second book would be possible. But thus far, there was nothing to convince her that it would ever come to pass.

"I had no idea truthfully what kind of reception it would get," she explained in *School Library Journal*. "If indeed it would ever get published, because I never looked to publish before. I knew how difficult it would be and I was a completely unknown writer."

One day a letter arrived in the mail. Joanne could tell immediately it was from one of the agents she had sent a copy of Harry to. She was thrilled to get a response. But as she tore open the envelope . . .

"I assumed it was a rejection note," she recalled in the *Daily Telegraph*. "But inside the envelope there was a letter saying 'Thank you. We would be pleased to represent your manuscript on an exclusive basis.' It was the best letter of my life. I read it eight times."

Christopher Little was an all-business, bottom-line kind of person. But this unsolicited manuscript by a totally unknown writer had touched him. It was very well written, the story was entertaining and, like Joanne, he sensed that *Harry Potter and the Sorcerer's Stone* was not merely a children's book.

Upon meeting her, Christopher Little was also impressed with her enthusiasm and her struggles against formidable odds to get the book written. He liked her grasp of reality. From his experience, Mr. Little knew that most children's authors struggle to make £2,000 ($4,000) a year and that they rarely wind up being well known.

"When I went into this, my agent said to me, 'I don't want you going away from this meeting thinking you're going to make a fortune,' " she reported to *School Library Journal*. "Then I said to him, 'I know I'm not going to make any money out of it. I know I'm not going to be famous.' All I ever wanted was for somebody to publish Harry so I could go to bookshops and see it."

Mr. Little began sending out *Harry Potter and the Sorcerer's Stone* to some of the biggest publishers in England. And as he had predicted, it was a long, hard road to being published. Before long, the first of a seemingly endless stream of rejections arrived at her agent's door. Some of the reasons given for not wanting to publish the book were that it was too long, too slow, or too literary. Joanne was disappointed but was encouraged by Mr. Little's assessment that the book was too good not to be picked up at some point.

Joanne went about her business of being a mother and a teacher and tried to put the chilly reception to Harry out of her thoughts. But during the next year, she would often find herself daydreaming about spying her book in the front window of the local bookshop. During those moments she would find herself smiling at the events in her life that had brought her to this moment.

In 1996, *Harry Potter and the Sorcerer's Stone* finally found a home with British publisher Bloomsbury Press. Joanne was beside herself with joy when she heard the news. "It was comparable only to having my daughter."

True to Mr. Little's prediction, Bloomsbury offered the modest amount of £2,000.

"That was totally okay with me," she once revealed of her reaction to Bloomsbury's acceptance of Harry. "All I wanted was to be able to support myself writing so I wouldn't have to give it up."

As often happens in the publishing industry, word of mouth about the merit of *Harry Potter and the Sorcerer's Stone* was good. Within months of Bloomsbury's purchase of the book, inquiries from publishers all over the world began pouring in.

In 1997, the overwhelming interest in this children's book by an unknown writer had reached such a level that an auction was arranged at the time of the annual Bologna, Italy, Book Fair (an annual book industry get-together in which foreign rights to books are sold). Joanne had been so thrilled at the prospect of Harry being published in her native England that she had paid only scant attention to what had been going on elsewhere in the world.

But she laughed when she recalled in *Salon* magazine the night her telephone rang around eight. It was Mr. Little calling long distance from New York.

"He said there was an auction taking place. An auction? I thought 'Sotheby's, Christie's [famous antiques auction house]?' Antiques? What is this all about? Then I realized that it was my book that was being auctioned off."

At that very moment, thousands of miles away in a crowded room at the Bologna Book Fair, editorial director Arthur A. Levine was about to take the biggest gamble of his life. The bidding on *Harry Potter and the Sorcerer's Stone* had been intense and the amounts being put up for the U.S. rights had already reached astronomical heights. Levine, a spirited man with a ready smile, was about to make a bid that could change his life forever.

"It's a scary thing when you keep bidding and the stakes are getting higher and higher," said Levine in *The New York Times*. "It's one thing to say I love this first novel by this unknown woman in Scotland and I want to publish it. It's another thing as the bidding goes higher. Do you love it this much? Do you love it at $50,000? At $70,000?"

The reason for Levine's concern was that the bidding was back to him and he was faced with the decision of offering an unheard-of bid of $100,000. "I had never paid so much for an acquisition before. It was a great risk. If people believe in you and you flop, then you walk out on the plank and plunge."

Little called Joanne again at ten that same evening. "He said I should get ready because a Mr. Levine of the Scholastic Press would pay a six-figure sum for the book and would be ringing me in a little bit. I nearly died."

The tension mounted in Joanne's tiny Edinburgh flat. She was excited and scared all at the same time. She had hoped, under ideal circumstances, that a modest U.S. sale would allow her to continue to write and teach on a part-time basis. But, she reasoned, things seemed to be moving much faster than anybody had expected.

The telephone rang promptly at eleven P.M. At the other end of the line, Levine was determined not to put any undue pressure on his new author. But his voice was shaking with excitement as he said hello.

"I called her very late," he told *The New York Times*, "and we had a very nice conversation. I said 'Don't be scared,' and she said, 'Thanks, I am.' And we both said now that we've paid this much, we had to concentrate on making the book work."

It was well past midnight when Joanne, after checking on her sleeping daughter, finally went to bed. "But I couldn't sleep. On one level, I was obviously delighted," she told a *Salon* magazine reporter. "But most of me was just frozen in terror."

7

HARRY CONQUERS
THE WORLD

Joanne had good reason to be fearful in the weeks following her big signing with Scholastic Books.

The amount of money involved was so unheard of in children's book circles that the book publishing gossip was that Arthur Levine and Scholastic had taken leave of their senses. Many doomsayers predicted that no matter how good the book was, it would certainly not make anywhere near enough to earn back the massive advance.

Joanne's agent and Arthur Levine assured her that Scholastic Books was not in the habit of laying out huge amounts of money for books they felt would fail. Joanne was not completely convinced. But that was only part of her concern.

Word of this author who had landed an advance unheard of for a children's book had quickly spread around the world. The normally shy woman was now being deluged with requests for interviews and her picture was appearing in newspapers and magazines. And this was before her book was even published in Great Britain.

If it had been up to her, Joanne would have done no publicity for the book at all. But she felt a strong sense of loyalty to those who had taken this chance with her, so she said yes to every request.

"The stakes had seemed to have gone up a lot," she told an interviewer in 1999 of those exciting days following her signing with Scholastic Press in the United States. "I attracted a lot of publicity for which I was totally unprepared."

Joanne was not big on change, and the idea of doing interviews in stuffy hotel rooms and television studios ran contrary to her nature. So when she started entertaining the press, she would gently insist that, whenever possible, interviews be done at her familiar table in the Nicholson Café.

When these interviews took place, a crowd of waiters and waitresses would stand on the periphery listening. They would smile as Joanne told how she would sit at this very table and write under the most trying of situations. Many of them had served her when she was down on her luck. Now they were as proud as they could possibly be that their regular customer was a well-known author.

Initially, she was not comfortable doing interviews. Joanne was not always smooth in her responses and worried about the kind of impression she was making. But she knew only how to be honest, and the press were going to make of that what they would.

Much of that early publicity put Joanne on the defensive. In many newspaper and magazine interviews, the reporters painted a picture of Joanne as a penniless, divorced single mother living on welfare and writing at her leisure in cafés. She had no problem with the accuracy, and yes, it was true.

But she felt "knocked sideways" by the negative image it presented of her and the fact that it was forcing her to relive what she considered one of the saddest moments of her life.

Joanne was quick to clarify that she had been gainfully employed since 1990, when she started writing Harry, and that the only reason she had to go on welfare was that the system in Edinburgh would not allow for child care. And then, she insisted, it was only for the year that she was completing the book.

As *Harry Potter and the Sorcerer's Stone* was going through the publishing process in England, Joanne found that there was one more compromise she was being asked to make. The publishers, fearful that a book with a woman's name on the cover might not attract young boys, asked if Joanne would mind if she were listed as J. K. Rowling. Joanne thought it was an odd request but saw no harm in going along with the notion.

Harry Potter and the Sorcerer's Stone was published in England in 1997. The book was an immediate smash, selling more than 150,000 copies in a matter of months. Reviewers fell over themselves in praise of the book.

One critic stated: "The book is an unassailable stand for the power of fresh, innovative storytelling." Another offered: "Rowling's ability to put a fantastic spin on sports, student rivalry, and eccentric faculty contributes to the humor, charm, and delight of her utterly captivating story."

By the end of the year, *Harry Potter and the Sorcerer's Stone* had gathered up a number of prestigious book awards, including the Nestlé Smarties Book Prize, the Federation of Children's Books Group Award and the British Book Awards Children's Book of the Year. Into 1998, the book had reached the total of a half million copies sold, an unheard-of number for a children's book.

Joanne was thrilled and more than a bit amused at what was happening with Harry. She was hard-pressed to answer the question she often asked as a child. Why? "I suppose it's mainly word of mouth," she offered of the book's success in the London *Guardian*. "I think children just tell one another about it."

But she did have a good laugh at the notion that the reason so many books were being sold was because a good many of them were being snapped up by adults just as eager to read the adventures of Harry as their children. As an example, she cited a story she had heard from a friend who had seen a man in a suit on a train reading a copy behind his newspaper.

"I had not aimed the books at children," she once said. "I only wrote them for me."

With the money from her U.S. book deal and another eight countries rolling in, Joanne was slowly beginning to adjust to the idea of not being poor. Oh, it did not come in one big gulp. She agonized for a long time whether to purchase a $100 coat so that she would look proper for her television appearances.

But with the success of *Harry Potter and the Sorcerer's Stone* in England and the American edition due out shortly, Joanne decided it was time to leave poverty behind her. The first thing she did was rent a house in Edinburgh. Nothing fancy. Just well-lighted rooms, heat, and comfortable furniture. However, for Joanne, it was pure heaven and relief. "I no longer have the constant worry of whether Jessica will outgrow a pair of shoes before I've got the money for the next pair," she sighed in a *Daily Telegraph* story.

Joanne was already hard at work on the follow-up to *Harry Potter and the Sorcerer's Stone* before the first book was published. So when she was not handling the increasing demand for interviews or tending to her daughter, Joanne was turning out pages of what would ultimately be titled *Harry Potter and the Chamber of Secrets*. But while she was now able to afford a computer and Jessica was of an age where she was spending part of the day in preschool, little of Joanne's approach to writing had changed.

Every day, after kissing her daughter goodbye, Joanne would walk down to Nicholson's Café, pull up a chair at a table facing out an upstairs window, pull out paper and a pen, and begin writing. The first time she did this after her first book had been accepted, the waiter, who had served her regularly when she was down and out, did a double take when she asked for a menu. One reason for continuing the routine was that Joanne felt lonely at the prospect of sitting in her house, by herself, in front of a computer.

"Writing and cafés are strongly linked in my brain," she recently proclaimed to the press. "I still write in longhand. I like physically shuffling around with papers."

Harry Potter and the Chamber of Secrets was almost complete and ready for publication when the U.S. edition of *Harry Potter and the Sorcerer's Stone* was brought out in August 1998. The British mania for Harry Potter was soon duplicated in the United States as children and adults fell in love with Harry and his adventures.

In short order, editions of Joanne's first book were coming out in nearly thirty other countries. Joanne would have a giggle at the different languages and, in some cases, the different covers her story was published with. As each new edition was released, her happiness increased.

Publishers on both sides of the Atlantic were now convinced that Harry Potter was no fluke, so contracts were quickly drawn up that would have Joanne writing a total of seven Harry Potter books in the coming years. Joanne was thrilled. Then she was scared to death.

In a practical sense, the longevity of the contract meant she would never want for anything for her daughter or herself. But there was also what she described as "a few weeks of terror" as she contemplated whether she could write the remainder of the books with the same enthusiasm now that the whole world was looking over her shoulder.

To relieve the fear of writer's block, Joanne sat down and plotted out the remaining five Harry Potter books. She was painstaking in figuring out the story lines, the specific elements of each adventure, and the important message that readers young and old would take away from each book. At the end of this plotting session, Joanne emerged confident in her ability to finish Harry Potter's education.

"And I finally realized what the most important thing for me was," she stated in *The Boston Globe*. "I love writing these books. I don't think anyone could enjoy reading them more than I enjoy writing them."

Harry Potter and the Chamber of Secrets was published in July 1998 and, like its predecessor, was an immediate sensation all over the world. In Great Britain alone, the book outsold the latest novels by adult writers John Grisham and Tom Clancy.

Joanne continued to be amazed at the way people had taken Harry Potter and his world into their hearts and minds. But the writer was also finding that having bestselling books was also beginning to complicate her life. Already well into writing the third book, *Harry Potter and the Prisoner of Azkaban*, Joanne was finding that she had less time to write because of interviews, book signings, and the odd lectures and school appearances.

Joanne was a good sport when it came to things like that. In the case of the book signings and appearances at schools, she loved the idea of actually meeting with the children who were reading her books. "As an ex-teacher, it's just so liberating to go in front of a class simply to entertain them and it's great when they've read the books and can quote you passages and know the characters," she said in *The Guardian*.

But there were also those days when things did not go according to plan and Joanne found herself overwhelmed to the point of tears. During what seemed like an endless round of promotional duties surrounding the release of *Harry Potter and the Chamber of Secrets*, Joanne was having trouble checking out of a London hotel. At first the hotel would not allow her to check out because there was no record of her name in the computer. Finally a hotel manager found her name but insisted that she could not leave until she paid her bill. This upset the normally unflappable Joanne because she knew that her publisher had already paid the bill. With the hotel fiasco finally straightened out, she hopped in a taxi, already late for an interview. Halfway there, Joanne realized that she had left the hotel without her purse.

It was all too much. Joanne burst into tears, startling the cabdriver.

However, most days her good humor and sunny outlook got Joanne through the difficulty of being in the public eye. She felt incredibly fortunate to be in this position because it had come as a result of her unwillingness to give up on her dream. So, yes, she would give interviews and talk to people about Harry until the cows came home.

But at the end of the day she would happily race home to comfort Jessica. As she held her young daughter and asked about her day at school, Joanne was proud—proud that as her mother, she was able to provide Jessica with security and a good life.

And if there was time, Joanne would walk down to Nicholson's Café, where she might find a few moments to write. She would sometimes order the usual espresso and water. But just as often she would also pick up the menu . . .

And think about getting something to eat.

8

HARRY EVER AFTER

H*arry Potter and the Prisoner of Azkaban* was released late in 1998. The mania for Harry continued as the book immediately followed its predecessors to the top of the world's bestseller lists.

Reporters once again came around, hoping the quiet author of these fantastic adventures would have a reason for Harry Potter's continued success. And once again Joanne found it hard to come up with an answer that did not have the words "shocked and amazed" somewhere in it.

Happily, Joanne was more than willing to try. "I am still stunned that I went from being an unknown writer on the breadline to having my books at the top of the charts. It's truly amazing," she would regularly tell reporters.

But all the news was not good. A number of religious groups had decided that Harry Potter books were promoting evil thoughts and ideas. Many of these groups sent letters to newspapers protesting the books, and in some cases, they tried to get the books removed from libraries and bookstores.

Joanne was upset by their actions but chose to ignore them. Eventually the storm of protest passed.

Joanne celebrated New Year's Eve 1999 quietly with a small group of friends. At the stroke of midnight, she toasted her good fortune and her good friends. She could only imagine what the upcoming year would offer.

A resolution was not long in coming. Nobody had ever referred to Joanne as a workaholic. But as fast as the new Harry books were coming out, one had to wonder if Joanne did anything but write. She repeatedly stated that writing was the thing she most liked to do. However, she did decide that she owed it to herself and Jessica to get away every once in a while. So she began traveling, taking short jaunts to neighboring countries that would allow Jessica and her to see the sights and get away from the distractions that were always a phone call away in Edinburgh.

It came as no surprise that Hollywood was soon wild about Harry as well. Moviemakers immediately saw the possibilities of Harry Potter as a movie. No fewer than a dozen film studios were actively pursuing the rights to turn Harry Potter into a full-length motion picture. Once again, Joanne was hanging by the telephone as Christopher Little relayed the latest messages regarding a film contract. But the negotiation of film deals, unlike that of book deals, tends to drag on for a long time, so Joanne was content to go about the business of writing the fourth installment of Harry Potter.

With two books out in the same year, Joanne

was given more time to turn out this latest adventure. There had been some concern by the publishers that writing two books literally back-to-back might have put a bit of a strain on their favorite author. However, Joanne was nothing if not anxious, after the seemingly endless round of press and publicity, to get back to creating another exciting Harry Potter adventure for her legion of fans.

The routine remained pretty much the same. Although her notoriety had made the Nicholson Café a sudden tourist attraction, and Joanne would occasionally find herself feeling self-conscious at being gawked at by people who had come to watch her work, she would still find time to sit and work there a few hours just about every day. But out of necessity, she was also working in other cafés and pubs, which she wisely refused to name.

Wherever she went, the writing continued to go smoothly. The characters had become like a second family to her. She knew what would work and what would appear false. Creating new names for her otherworldly characters was always a joy. But Joanne had to admit that with this book, things were beginning to change. Harry and the other characters were now well into their teen years. She felt it was time to have Harry discover girls.

This was an exciting turn of events for Joanne, one that allowed her to revisit her own adolescence as a blueprint for how Harry should react the first time he notices a girl as something other than a good buddy. Harry was never boring, but now there was an extra bit of excitement that would have her snatching up her pen and paper at every opportunity.

Shortly before the turn of the New Year 2000, Joanne, with Jessica by her side, boarded an airplane at London's Heathrow Airport, headed for the United States on a three-week book tour. These were exciting times for Joanne. She had heard about how well the first three books had done in America, but she was anxious to meet with her readers face-to-face and to see the joy and excitement they had for her work in their eyes.

At each and every stop on this cross-country tour, Joanne was very much the teacher in her dealings with the thousands of fans who lined up to see her. She would encourage them to read and write as often as possible. She would chuckle at the inevitable question on how to pronounce her name before saying, "It's Roe-ling, not Row-ling." The woman of simple tastes even got to like the rock-star treatment she was getting with limo rides and big security at every stop. The look on Joanne's face was worth a thousand words. But only one was really necessary . . .

Joy.

The year 2000 would bring continued success for Joanne. *Harry Potter and the Goblet of Fire* was in place for a July 8, 2000, publication date. It was also announced during this period that Warner Bros. had captured the rights to make the movie version of *Harry Potter and the Sorcerer's Stone*. Originally the studio had stated that Steven Spielberg was interested in directing the film. But the director would later bow out of the project, saying "My directorial interests were taking me in another direction." Eventually the studio made its choice and assigned a talented director, Chris Columbus, and a screenwriter, Steven Kloves, to adapt Joanne's fantasy world to the screen.

Joanne agreed to the Warner Bros. offer on the

condition that she would have input into the screenplay and that the movie would be live action rather than animation. But as the studio officially announced that Harry Potter would be in theaters in the summer of 2001, she had to admit to being nervous about the prospect of seeing Harry on the big screen. "It's actually a mixture of excitement and nervousness," she offered upon hearing the good news, in a Web site chat. "I do think Harry would make a great film. But obviously I do feel protective toward the characters I've lived with so long."

In March, director Columbus flew to Scotland, where he and Joanne met. Both came away from the meeting enthusiastic about the film "I'm terribly excited," said Columbus in the *Los Angeles Times*. "My oldest daughter, Eleanor, who is ten, got me into the books over a year ago. Between my four kids and their friends, I've heard a lot about what this movie should be and how I could ruin it if I cut this or that scene. I won't let anyone down. It will be a faithful adaptation."

Joanne was also in good spirits about her sudden involvement in the movie business. "I'm more involved than I thought I would be. I can't wait to see how they will pull off a Quidditch game."

The publicity campaign for the release of *Harry Potter and the Goblet of Fire* reached massive proportions as the days counted down to the official publication date. At this point, Joanne was not looking forward to answering a lot of the same questions yet again; she had in recent months started saying no to all but the most important outlets just so she would have time to write.

Her publishers took the hint and, in late spring, announced that Joanne would do one ninety-minute interview session in London and that would be it. Soon journalists from all over the world were flying in for the opportunity to ask the world's most popular author questions about her new book and her life in general.

Joanne was a bit nervous at the prospect of facing so many reporters at the same time and was concerned that this massive press conference would get out of control. Much of the press conference turned out to be predictable. There were the usual questions concerning why Harry had proven to be so popular, her struggles in Edinburgh, and how she was coping with success. Joanne fielded them with ease and responded, often with humor, concisely. But there were some surprise announcements along the way.

Joanne revealed that an important character would die in the fourth book and that Harry would develop his first crush on a girl. The author also offered that in the fifth book readers would finally discover why Harry continues to spend his summers with the frightful Dursleys.

The secretive author also offered that Harry's parents would not return and that she had decided long ago that magic could not bring back the dead. But she did hint that Harry's parents would continue to be an important part of future books.

She left the press conference relieved that the hard part of writing was once again behind her. Now she could get back to the fun part . . .

The writing itself.

Joanne would continue to be anxious as July 8 got closer and closer. At this point, nobody was betting against the fact that *Harry Potter and the*

Goblet of Fire would do as well, if not better, than her previous three books. But Joanne was never one to take anything for granted.

Finally the date had arrived and Joanne crossed her fingers as her latest Harry Potter adventure went on sale in England and the United States at the same time. Within hours, the first reports began to come in. Bookstores were selling out of copies in a matter of minutes and were already on the telephone to reorder. Within days, the book was high up on the bestseller charts around the world. Joanne heaved a sigh of relief at the news.

Because the magic of Harry Potter was still there.

Joanne moved through the end of summer in a state of grace. She was already hard at work at the next Harry book. She was happy and healthy, and she had a wonderful daughter to boot.

But with the beginning of book number five, the end was now in sight. Harry Potter would graduate from his seven years of schooling at Hogwarts some time around the year 2003. And although she would occasionally tease about never saying never when asked if she would follow Harry off to college, the author has remained adamant that Harry Potter will end with book number seven.

She has admitted to feeling sad at the idea that Harry will someday end and feels that it will be a "bereavement" when she has written the last line on the final page. But she insists that "there will be no Harry Potter's midlife crisis or Harry Potter as an old wizard."

But as she closes in on the end of the year 2000, Joanne could not be happier. Her life has exceeded her expectations. She has a beautiful daughter and she is making a living doing what she loves to do. And she is not sad at the fact that there is no man in her life. Her feeling on that topic is that if Mr. Perfect were to come along, she would be thrilled.

"But it's not my top priority," she told *Salon* magazine. "Right now my life is very fulfilled."

While her future after Harry Potter is still up in the air, the author knows that it will center on writing. It is all she knows, and she feels putting pen to paper is necessary for her. Joanne once admitted that "I don't feel normal when I haven't written for a while."

Joanne has hinted many times that her next step after Harry would be to write more adult novels. But she is honest enough to realize that she will probably never write anything as popular as Harry, and that is all right with her.

"I will have lived with Harry for thirteen years and I know I'll probably have to take some time off to grieve. But then I'll be on with the next book."

What that will be is anybody's guess, including Joanne's. But she knows where she will go for inspiration. "I might just get on another train."

9

TOUCHED BY
AN ANGEL

Two dramas were unfolding in July 1999. In her Edinburgh, Scotland, home, Joanne was working day and night in an attempt to finish *Harry Potter and the Goblet of Fire*. She was refusing all interview requests and avoiding any distractions that would keep her from finishing the long anticipated fourth adventure of Harry Potter.

The fame and celebrity status that had grown up around Joanne had caused her to alter her writing routine. Her phone rang constantly, interrupting her quiet time in the room in her house that doubled as her office and writing room. And though she continued to spend much of each day writing at the table of her favorite outdoor restaurant, Nicholson's, word had gotten out and she was often interrupted by sightseers requesting a photo or an autograph. Eventually she began writing in other restaurants around town in an attempt to find the time to finally finish *Goblet of Fire*. Joanne was finding that dealing with fame was not always easy.

At the same time, in Toronto, Canada, nine-year-old Natalie McDonald was dying of leukemia.

Natalie was the ultimate Harry Potter fan. She lived and breathed Joanne's stories from the beginning, and it was Harry Potter's flights of fantasy that had helped the young girl cope with her pain and her illness. A family friend, Annie Kidder, wanted to do something special to make Natalie's last days a bit more pleasant and felt that hearing from her favorite author would make the young girl deliriously happy.

Annie found the address for Joanne's London

publisher and sent a series of letters, E-mails, and faxes, explaining Natalie's dire situation and requesting some kind of response from the author. The people in the publishing office were touched by the sincerity of Annie's messages and, despite Joanne's strict order not to be disturbed as she raced to complete *Harry Potter and the Goblet of Fire,* they believed this heartfelt request was something she would want to respond to. Finally the latest letter from Annie Kidder was forwarded to Joanne's Edinburgh home.

Joanne was not there to receive it.

After an intense period of writing, Joanne felt she needed a break and so had decided, in mid July, to take a short vacation in Spain. Annie's letter had arrived the day after Joanne left. When she returned from her holiday, the first thing she read was the letter from Annie. She was touched and saddened at her young fan's illness and immediately felt compelled to do something to help.

"But I had a bad feeling that I was too late," she told *Maclean's.*

Joanne called Annie Kidder but she was not at home. She instantly dashed off a long letter and

E-mailed a copy to Natalie and her mother, Valerie. The E-mail arrived on August 4, 1999.

Sadly, Joanne would later discover that her message had arrived too late. Natalie had died on August 3.

But Annie would recall Joanne's kind words in that letter. She treated the dying young girl with respect and lovingly talked about her books and characters. In the body of that letter, Joanne also revealed the story and secrets of *Harry Potter and the Goblet of Fire,* a full eleven months before the book was to be released.

This might have been the end of a very sad story.

But Joanne had other ideas. The author, heartbroken by her inability to bring comfort to the young child's final days, had been so moved by Natalie and her life struggles and devotion to Harry Potter that she decided to honor the girl she had never met but writing her into a passage of *Harry Potter and the Goblet of Fire.* And so on page 159 of *Goblet of Fire,* Joanne created a scene in which the sorting hat sends first-year student Natalie McDonald to Harry's Gryffindor house. This would be the only time Joanne would ever use a real person's name in a Harry Potter book.

After receiving Joanne's letter to her daughter, Natalie's mother, Valerie, wrote back to thank the author for her efforts on behalf of her daughter. Joanne was touched by Valerie's letter, and a regular correspondence began between the two women. As the letters went back and forth between Canada and Scotland, Joanne found that she had discovered in Valerie a kindred spirit, someone, who like Joanne, had experienced the death of a loved one, and who felt strongly about the importance and challenges of motherhood.

As the time for publication of *Harry Potter and the Goblet of Fire* neared, Joanne and Valerie agreed to meet in England to cement their relationship face to face. And so in July 2000, Valerie, her husband, and two other daughters traveled to England to meet with Joanne.

Joanne was unsure how this meeting would go. She had always been a very private person and this kind of friendship was out of character for her. But the kindness and love expressed in their letters had found a special place in Joanne's heart and so she felt comfortable about meeting this woman.

The meeting between the two women was a joyous, bittersweet time. There were hugs all around, tears were shed in joy and happiness in the memory of a child whom Valerie had lost and Joanne had never known but, in a very spiritual sense, had come to know.

It was during their London visit that Valerie and her family, on a sightseeing excursion around the city on the London tube, discovered Joanne's secret memorial to Natalie. To pass the time on the tube, Valerie began reading *Harry Potter and the Goblet of Fire* to her daughters. One can only imagine the surprise when she turned to page 159 and discovered how Joanne had chosen to honor the memory of Natalie.

Natalie McDonald was in heaven. But in the heart and mind of Joanne Kathleen Rowling, she would forever live in Hogwarts.

10

THE HOGWARTS EXPRESS

A light blue car pulled to a stop at London's King's Cross Station on July 8, 2000. Inside, Joanne was still rubbing the sleep from her eyes at the early morning wakeup. She was already missing her daughter, Jessica, who would be sleeping soundly in the home of her sister, Di, as she prepared to catch a train.

Looking outside, Joanne saw a scene of total chaos. A literal army of photographers and reporters had lined the railway station entrance, television cameras jockeying for a good position, people being pushed and shoved every which way. Beyond the cluster of press people and behind a barricade stood more than three hundred children and their bewildered parents, who had braved the cold weather and the early hour for a chance to see their favorite author.

Sadly, while the photographers and reporters were given free rein to move wherever they wanted, the children were being kept in that one spot, making even a glimpse of Joanne all but impossible.

As she emerged from the car, a fresh-off-the-presses copy of *Harry Potter and the Goblet of Fire* clutched in her hands, a shout went up from a group of photographers, who begged: "Give us a wave, Jo!" For Joanne, it was a bit early in the morning for this sort of thing. But after a moment's hesitation, she rolled her eyes, presented a half smile–half grimace to the photographers, and offered up a halfhearted wave as the flashbulbs exploded around her like lightning.

"It's rather mad isn't it?" she joked with photographers as they snapped away. "I'd really like to talk to some children if I ever manage to finish with you lot."

With that, Joanne made a break through the crowd and instinctively made for the children. Sadly, she was intercepted by public relations people and ushered back toward the waiting cameras.

"I'm sorry," she yelled at the children as she was hustled away. "I'm not allowed."

Surrounded by personal assistants and representatives of her British publishing company, Joanne made her way through the station and to Platform 9¾. Where she came face to face with The Queen of Scots which, for the occasion, had been made over into a real life incarnation of The Hogwarts Express. The train, an old-fashioned, red, steam-powered engine not unlike the fictional train that takes Harry Potter to the School of Witchcraft and Wizardry, is pouring smoke out of its towering stack. Behind it, an observation car, a dining car, and a sleeping car are rapidly filling up with people. Joanne stops in front of the train and smiles gamely one last time for the photographers and steps aboard.

The Hogwarts Express will be Joanne's home for the next four days.

As part of a massive publicity stunt to kick off the official publication of *Harry Potter and the Goblet of Fire,* Joanne agreed to go on a train tour, beginning at London's King's Cross station and ending at Perth, Scotland. The train would make stops at train stations along the way and Joanne would sign books for a limited number of children, whose names were chosen in drawings sponsored by bookstores at bookstores, museums, or the train stations at each stop. It was a grand idea to help promote her new book, but Joanne saw the train ride as something much more important—an opportunity to meet her young readers face to face.

"I love meeting the child readers," she said in *Maclean's.* "They ask the best questions. The children talk about the characters as though they're mutual friends I happen to know a bit better."

Promptly at 11:27 A.M., the train began to slowly pull out of the station amid the crush of television cameras, news reporters and the number of children who had awakened as early as 4 A.M. just so they could get to the station and see their favorite author off. Joanne sensed her young fans' disappointment and stuck her head out the window and waved at the children.

"Oh God. I'm sorry. I'm sorry," she called out to the children. "It was nice meeting you all."

Joanne was saddened at what she considered the shabby treatment her young fans received, and at the same time, more than a bit overwhelmed by the enormous interest in her latest book. She vowed to make it up to the children at the first opportunity. As for all the cameras going off and the reporters treating every word that tumbled out of her mouth as gold, she did not know if she would ever get used to that.

Joanne took a quick tour of the train. She immediately fell in love with the dining car, whose plush brocade furnishings seemed fit for royalty and would offer her a wonderful view of the countryside as the train flew past. The dining car was decked out in antique elegance, a finery reserved for the kings and queens these cars had once carried. And, at the end of the day, the sleeping car would assuredly provide her pleasant dreams.

Amid darkening clouds and the promise of a

summer rain, the train left Knights Crossing and pulled steadily out of London, the cars beginning the steady rock and rattles that would be the trip's constant companion. Not too long after leaving Knights Crossing, the steam engine unceremoniously broke down and a modern-day diesel was recruited to tow the older train for the remainder of the trip.

Inside, Joanne had made herself comfortable and was beginning the first of many interviews with the members of the press on board. It was a time of reflection as she once again told the story of how Harry came to be, the latest news regarding the Harry Potter movie, and the behind-the-scenes stories of writing *Harry Potter and the Goblet of Fire*. And there were many new revelations. For the first time, Joanne candidly revealed that she had, in fact, been late completing the book, due in part to having scrapped the manuscript and started over when she realized that her presentation of the story and the characters was not consistent with the three previous books and would not reach the conclusion she wanted. And, for the first of many times, she tried to express her reaction to the continued worldwide popularity of the Harry Potter books.

"I can't explain it," she offered a reporter from the *New York Times* at one point. "I don't have an answer. I just write what I wanted to write. I write what amuses me. It's totally for myself. I never in my wildest dreams expected this popularity."

The first stop for The Hogwarts Express was a mid-afternoon signing at Didicot Railway Centre in the town of Didicot. That first night the train chugged into the Kidderminster Station in the Severen Valley. Joanne appreciated the logistics of the tour. The plan included big and small cities alike, and the trip was reminding Joanne of the old days when she traveled everywhere by train.

On the second day of the tour, the fantasy train stopped in the cities of Manchester and York. By the third day, the train had left Newcastle and had crossed over into Scotland and into her hometown of Edinburgh, where Joanne was greeted as a hometown hero.

It was the same at every stop. The train would pull into the station and Joanne would either be whisked away to a local bookstore, where she would meet a selected group of her fans and sign their books. Or, more often than not, she would meet and greet her admirers in the train station.

As always, Joanne put on her best smiling face despite the frequent early-morning stops on the schedule and the fact she readily had admitted in *Reader's Digest* that "I'm really not a morning person." But nothing, including the fact that she was already missing Jessica, would stop her from being the embodiment of all her fans fantasies . . . even if only for a moment.

And at each stop, there were wondrous stories of the lengths that many of her fans went to get an audience with Joanne. A twelve-year-old boy won a coveted ticket to meet Joanne by winning a complex Harry Potter trivia quiz. Upon hearing that a London bookstore was giving away tickets, one persistent girl awoke at 4 A.M. and was in line outside the bookstore at 6:30 A.M., hours before the store was due to open. Still another young girl had sadly thought she had lost out on the drawing, but was miraculously rewarded with a ticket when one of the original winners gave up his ticket to attend a school athletic event.

And at each stop along the tour, the reaction from the children was always the same . . . shock, delight, amazement, and a sudden inability to speak. To finally get to meet the creator of their fantasies was, according to the description of the scene by an *Entertainment Weekly* reporter, "deliriously mind boggling."

The excitement generated by Joanne's appearances was best summed up by one ten-year-old who emerged from a brief meeting with Joanne and exclaimed, "Am I allowed to faint now?"

Finally, on the fourth day, The Hogwarts Express pulled into the railroad station in Perth, Scotland. Joanne was both relieved and excited that this was the last stop on her book tour. She greeted this last group of anxious fans with a broad smile and a respectful attitude. As she signed this last batch of books, she was able to ask each child about what they liked about the books and who their favorite character was. At one point, a child was asked to pose with Joanne for a photograph.

The child appeared a bit nervous at being pushed into the spotlight, but Joanne calmed him when she jokingly said, "Pretend like you're thrilled to see me."

Finally, with the last book signed, Joanne got into a car for a sixty-minute ride back to her house in Edinburgh. During the ride back, she looked out the window at the passing scenery and reflected on the turn her life had taken. In the past year, she had been named by the prestigious *Forbes* Magazine one of the top twenty-five most powerful celebrities in the world. In June 2000, she had made a quick trip to Dartmouth College in New Hampshire, where she received her first honorary degree. But easily a high point came to Joanne in the past month when she was summoned to Buckingham Palace, where she was awarded The Order Of The British Empire by the royal family.

There were other, more personal memories to relive. There was the joy in watching Jessica grow into quite the wonderful young girl, turning six and entering school. Because she did not feel Jessica had been old enough to comprehend the world of Harry Potter, Joanne had decided that she would not begin to read the stories to her until her daughter turned age seven. But what she discovered is that the children in her daughter's class were already quite familiar with her work and so they were constantly coming up to Jessica and asking her questions about Harry that she did not have the answers to.

"She didn't have an idea what they were all about," Joanne once explained to *Entertainment Weekly*. "And I just thought, 'I'm excluding her from this huge part of my life, and it's making her an outsider.' So I read them to her and she became completely Harry Potter obsessed."

And there were the obvious changes that had taken place in her own life as the result of the worldwide popularity of Harry Potter. She had more money than she ever dreamed of having. But she spent wisely, insuring a wonderful life for Jessica and herself. But the added attention was not always welcome. Before her Harry Potter books became a global sensation, Joanne was still able to move about Edinburgh without being recognized and could still spend hours writing at her favorite café, while listening to good music and sipping from a seemingly bottomless cup of coffee.

But with the publication of the third Harry Potter book, *Harry Potter and the Prisoner of Azkaban,* Joanne began to notice an increasing lack of privacy. With her writing habits now well publicized, she soon began to be the center of attention as she would write at an outside table of a cafe. And although people were always pleasant when approaching her, it would often conflict with what she insisted on being her ideal writing day.

"In an ideal day, I'll work six to ten hours," she told a Knight Ridder News Service reporter. "But now I'm fighting to get the time to write. I use cafes like offices and I try to get away from the house whenever possible."

But with her notoriety, Joanne had found herself spending more and more time writing at home. And even that did not protect her from regular interruptions.

"There was a phase when I had journalists at my front door quite a lot," she related to a *Newsweek* reporter. "And that was quite horrible. That was not something I had ever anticipated happening to me, and it's not pleasant."

But, like every other element of her newfound celebrity, Joanne had learned to deal with it. Which is why she took things like this just-concluded publicity trip in support of *Harry Potter and the Goblet of Fire* in stride. The town of Edinburgh was rounding into view. Joanne saw the familiar streets and buildings. In a short time, she would be taking Jessica in her arms and holding her tight.

Joanne Kathleen Rowling was the most famous author on the planet. But tonight she would just be Mom.

For the next couple of months, Joanne would once again return to normal pursuits. Every morning she would walk Jessica to school and pick her up at the end of the day. And she would find time to do some window shopping along Edinburgh's Princess Street. She also did more interviews, a handful of appearances in bookstores in and around London and, to spare Jessica somewhat from the constant questions of classmates, Joanne did a pair of lectures as a reward for the two top performing classes in her daughter's school.

Joanne also began to turn her attention to charitable causes. She agreed to become the spokeswoman for the National Council for One Parent Families and donated $725,000 to the charity, whose emphasis was on helping single mothers. This was obviously a cause that was near and dear to Joanne's heart.

"I had a degree, a profession, and friends who were willing to lend me money when I badly needed it," she said in a speech before the organization. "So if I met obstacles pulling myself out of the benefits system, how much more difficult must it be for people who don't have the same advantages? Seven years after becoming a lone parent, I feel qualified to look anyone I meet in the eye and say that people bringing up children single-handedly deserve not condemnation, but congratulation."

Joanne's charitable outlook also led to her establishing a Harry Potter Fund with the charity group Comic Relief U.K., an organization dedicated to helping children in England and Africa.

Finally, when she had a few moments to herself, she secretly began writing the fifth Harry Potter book, *Harry Potter and the Order of the Phoenix.*

"I literally don't feel quite right if I haven't written for a while," she confessed during a *Newsweek* interview. "A week is about as long as I can go without getting extremely edgy. It really is a compulsion."

As summer began to turn to fall, Joanne realized that the quiet times were about to end and that she would soon be giving a reading before the largest audience she could ever imagine. The odyssey that would take her to Canada had begun almost a year earlier when she was racing to complete *Harry Potter and the Goblet of Fire.*

"I was feeling very fraught at the time," she told a Canadian Broadcast Corporation interviewer. "I was halfway through book four and I said yes. At that point, I did say yes to quite a lot of things just to stop people from asking me anything else because I really wanted to be writing. Then I sort of emerged from the madness that had been book four."

And realized exactly what she had said yes to.

As part of the festivities of the Vancouver International Writers' Festival, Joanne had agreed to do a pair of readings in the famed Pacific Coliseum in front of a projected sold-out audience of six thousand. But when word had leaked out that Joanne would be attending, the demand for tickets was so great that the festival directors had come back to Joanne with the request that she give an additional reading the day before in the Toronto Sky Dome, the home of the Toronto Blue Jays baseball team, in front of a projected twenty thousand young fans.

"I realized how big the reading was going to be and then I got terrified," she told the CBC interviewer.

Once she got over her initial fears, Joanne was thrilled at the prospect of going to Canada for the first time. The writer had always had a warm feeling about the country and its people and was looking forward to experiencing both "up close and personal" in what would be a six-day visit.

Joanne first flew into New York City, where she spent a couple of days meeting with her American publisher and giving a handful of magazine and newspaper interviews. Some of the questions covered familiar ground, but a few odd things had popped up in the wake of the publication of *Harry Potter and the Goblet of Fire* that she needed to address. One of the most outrageous to Joanne's many readers was the fact that, in the final sequence of the fourth book, there was a mistake in the order that Harry's parents emerge from Voldemort's wand. In the previous three books Joanne had said on several occasions that Voldemort had killed James first and Lily second. But in *Goblet of Fire* we are told that the ghosts would emerge in reverse order in which James steps out of the wand before Lily. Joanne exclaimed that it was just an unfortunate editing error that would be corrected in later editions of the book.

She was also questioned about why she was two months late in handing in the final manuscript of *Harry Potter and the Goblet of Fire*. She conceded that the book had been the hardest one to write and, while she had always taken great pains to be consistent in her story elements, that the plot basically got away from her.

"I wrote what I thought was half the book and

suddenly realized that there was this huge, gaping hole in the middle of the plot," she explained to *Entertainment Weekly*. "The whole profile of the books got so much higher since the third book and there was an edge of external pressure."

Joanne explained that the problem arose when she had to pull a girl character, a Weasley cousin, because she had discovered that this character was serving the same function as investigative journalist, Rita Skeeter.

Joanne was sorry if the delays or other editorial errors confused her readers and assured them that more care would be taken with future books.

Joanne arrived in Toronto on October 22, 2000. Her first order of business would be something personal. She had been in contact with Valerie McDonald and had arranged to spend some time with the McDonald family and Annie Kidder on that first day. After arriving in Toronto, to no small amount of fanfare, and checking into her hotel, Joanne met with the McDonald family and Annie and spent what she would later state was a "wonderful" afternoon of sightseeing at Niagara Falls. But while this time with friends put her in an upbeat mood, the fear of doing a reading in front of an estimated 20,000 adoring fans once again was on her mind.

"I'm so terrified," she told the Knight Ridder News Service the day before the reading. "I'm not The Rolling Stones. How is this going to work?"

The day before the Sky Dome reading was taken up with a number of interviews and meeting representatives of her Canadian publisher. Joanne rather enjoyed meeting the press in Canada and patiently explained how her life had changed in the past few months since the publication of *Harry Potter and the Goblet of Fire*, retold some old stories about her early life that suddenly seemed fresh again, and dropped a few hints about the fifth Harry Potter book, already in progress.

During that busy day, Joanne also found the time to do some charitable works by appearing at a fund-raising luncheon for the Toronto Public Library. And despite signs stating that no autographs would be given during the luncheon, Joanne once again missed a meal when she willingly greeted and signed books for a steady stream of children who approached her.

But the main point of interest continued to be the Sky Dome reading scheduled for October 24. Ticket sales had been reportedly brisk for the event and an estimated twenty thousand fans would be in attendance. Joanne would acknowledge that she was delighted to be addressing so many of her fans at one time, but that there was still a lot of nervousness at the notion of reading Harry in the middle of a huge baseball field.

"I'm kind of looking at it like, if I can get through this, I can get through anything."

Joanne awoke the day of the reading with butterflies in her stomach. It was her big day.

The Sky Dome reading had been planned around a circus atmosphere. Children entering the stadium, many of whom were dressed as their favorite Harry Potter characters, were greeted by light shows and slide shows that projected elements of Harry Potter lore up on screens throughout the stadium as well as an indoor fireworks display. A group of outlandishly clothed wizards wandered through the stadium, performing magic tricks.

Prior to Joanne's appearance, a pair of Canadian children's authors, Tim Wynne Jones and Kenneth Oppel, read selections from their most recent books. But it was obvious that the young fans in the stands were far more interested in hearing Joanne.

Finally the event announcer stepped to the podium. Before he could even get out her name, the crowd erupted in a wave of applause and cheers. The moment had arrived. The stadium lights dimmed and Joanne moved to a podium in the center of the stadium and stood in the glare of a lone spotlight as the crowd went wild. The applause and cheers went on for some minutes as Joanne stood smiling and somewhat shocked at the response.

The thunderous applause continued as Joanne stepped up to the microphone.

"Thank you," she said, her voice echoing through the stadium. "I'm delighted and terrified to be here."

The crowd went silent.

Joanne took out her copy of *Harry Potter and the Goblet of Fire,* laid it on the podium, opened it to chapter four, and began to read. Almost immediately, her young fans, many of whom had brought their own copy of the new book, did likewise and began to read silently along with her.

Her stagefright now magically gone, Joanne, reading clearly and occasionally adding dramatic voices and accents, brought life to passages in her book in which the Dursleys are visited by an assortment of wizards. The children sat wide-eyed and enraptured. Many had tears streaming down their faces. For them, this was truly a magic time.

Fourteen minutes after she began reading, Joanne was finished. She closed her book as the cheers once again cascaded down around her. For the next fifteen minutes, she offered up answers to the most frequently asked questions about Harry Potter and his world. She finished by thanking the audience for coming and stepped off the stage to thunderous applause and the voice of the announcer urging the children to "read, read, read."

Joanne was deliriously happy as she stepped from the stage, receiving congratulations from friends and associates for a job well done. She was literally on a cloud the next two days as she journeyed to Vancouver, where she gave two more spirited readings before two sold-out audiences at Vancouver's famed Pacific Coliseum and, whenever possible, reached out to the children who would shyly approach her.

Prior to those readings, Joanne once again sat down with a group of reporters, and she stated her reason for agreeing to do a large reading like the one at the Sky Dome. She admitted that she would prefer the one-on-one contact that small readings and bookstore signings provided but that, sadly, those days appeared to be gone forever.

" 'If I did that now, I would never see my daughter," she said in a story that appeared on the Harry Potter fandom Web site. "I would never write another book. I would never eat or sleep. So I have to cut my cloth. I can say, 'Well, I won't read anymore,' which I would really miss. Or I could do bigger readings where I reach more people at once and that's the way I've chosen to go."

And while she told the assembled reporters that she considers book signings "a bottomless pit" that often test her mental and emotional strength, she willingly does them and for one big reason.

"I've never had a rude child, which for me is

incredible. Never had one throw a tantrum. I've never had a child ask for more than I can give. Never once had a child for which I didn't feel anything but affection."

Joanne patiently answered the expected questions about dealing with success and what the future holds for Harry Potter. Although she would not like to admit it, Joanne was getting tired. And so she was grateful when the final round of applause greeted her last night in Vancouver.

Joanne knew it was time to go home.

She was missing her daughter terribly and, after six days of total adoration, was looking forward to returning to the simple life of writing at her favorite café, taking Jessica to and from school, and maybe doing a little shopping.

However, as her plane winged back across the Atlantic, she also knew that there would be something else awaiting her. Something that both excited and scared her.

The movie version of *Harry Potter and the Sorcerer's Stone* had begun filming two weeks earlier. And she could not begin to guess how a whole new world of Harry Potter would unfold.

11

IT'S ONLY A MOVIE

Joanne had flown to Los Angeles early in 2000 to finalize the contracts for the movie version of *Harry Potter and the Sorcerer's Stone*. And for Joanne, seeing the place where movie magic was made was an eye-opening experience. The negotiations were conducted in a cordial, straightforward manner in which Joanne's wishes were considered and honored.

Joanne had been cautious in dealing with the movie people. She had heard all too many stories about books being totally distorted in their transition to the screen and was fearful of the same thing happening to Harry. But in the end, Joanne came away from those meetings secure in the fact that the movie version of her book would be true to the world she created.

Joanne was given the title of executive producer when the deal was finalized with Warner Bros. to make the movie version of *Harry Potter and the Sorcerer's* Stone. Knowing little about how the movie business worked, she did not think much of the title at first. But as the various elements of the movie began to fall into place, she was glad she had it.

Because, as these things often happen in Hollywood, suggestions were soon being made that would change *Harry Potter and the Sorcerer's Stone* into something other than what the book had been. Early on Steven Spielberg had been considered the front-runner to direct the film. And Joanne had been thrilled with the idea of having the famed director of such films as *E.T.* and *Jurassic Park* create the Harry Potter world.

But during a series of meetings between Spielberg and Joanne, some very different opinions came to the surface. The director wanted to make a movie that would be more American, rather than English, in tone. There was talk of making many of the students and teachers international. But Joanne strenuously objected on the grounds that doing that would mean inventing characters that were not in the book. Spielberg went so far as to suggest that child actor Hayley Joel Osment, an American, would be the perfect choice to play Harry.

In the end, Joanne and the director respectfully agreed to disagree, and Spielberg moved on to another project. There was immediate speculation that Joanne and the famous director did not get along personally. But Joanne, ever the diplomat, said that it ultimately boiled down to a question of whose vision would ultimately wind up on the screen.

"There were things he said that I didn't agree with," she told the *London Times*. "There were things he said I did agree with."

There were also questions raised early on about the kind of merchandising tie-ins that would accompany the release of the film. That there would be fast-food restaurant toys, lunch boxes, dolls, and fully licensed Harry Potter action figures associated with the movie was a sensitive issue with Joanne, who insisted that any merchandising connected with the film be tasteful and that a theme pushing literacy and reading be included. Warner Bros. was agreeable to much of what Joanne said— typified by the fact that Coca-Cola became an official sponsor of the film, but Harry would not be drinking a Coke in the film—and were in agreement that all associated items should be presented in a noncommercial manner.

Joanne insisted that, while she had basically sold the rights to let the studio do what they wanted, her opinion regarding the way Harry Potter was marketed had been taken into consideration by the studio. She had insisted, "Please trust me. I am fighting in your corner," when it came to how her creative "baby" was being sold.

"If the action figures are horrible, tell the kids I said don't buy them," she said in *Good Housekeeping*. The *New York Times* was also privy to the degree Joanne would defend her creation when she told them, "I would do anything to prevent Harry from turning up in fast-food boxes everywhere. I would do my utmost. That would be my worst nightmare."

A number of other directors were offered up to Rowling before Chris Columbus was finally named early in 2000 to direct the film. Columbus and Joanne were on the same page when it came to how *Harry Potter and the Sorcerer's Stone* should be portrayed on the screen. They both agreed that the film should be, like the book, very British in tone and that it should be populated by largely British actors.

But when it was announced that American screenwriter Steve Kloves had been chosen to write the script for the movie, Joanne immediately had second thoughts.

"The person I was most nervous about meeting by far was Steve Kloves," she related in an *Entertainment Weekly* interview. "I was really ready to hate him. This was the man who was gonna butcher my baby. The first time I met him, he said,

'You know who my favorite character is?' And I thought, 'You're gonna say Ron.' But he said 'Hermione.' I just kind of melted."

Not too long after receiving the assignment to write the script, Kloves told *Reader's Digest* what he loved about Harry. "From the first page of book one, she had me. There's a genuine edge and darkness to it, and one reason she's so popular with children is that there's no pandering whatsoever."

He would recall in later months how the cordial relationship between Joanne and himself worked during the writing of the *Sorcerer's Stone* script. He explained that much of the dialogue in the script was his variation on what Joanne had written in her book. In doing that, Kloves felt he was anticipating some elements of the ongoing Harry Potter story that would come into play in later books.

"She reacted strongly," he reflected, in an Ain't It Cool Web site interview. "She was like, 'Ah, you sensed something but you also missed something.' In one instance, I put something in, a reference to something. She said, 'That's great but you can't do that because something's going to happen in book five that makes that impossible . . ."

That Joanne would be such a stickler for details does not come as a surprise, because Harry Potter, in the ensuing years, had become much more than a fictional character. "I have known Harry and I have been writing about Harry for ten years," she explained to the *Los Angeles Times*. "He is very, very real to me."

The year 2000 found Joanne burning the candle at both ends, putting the finishing touches on *Harry Potter and the Goblet of Fire,* while monitoring the progress of Kloves's first draft of the script and sitting in on meetings on other aspects of the film-making process. With the director and writer in place, the next task was casting the film and, in particular, the all-important role of Harry Potter. The search for the perfect Harry was stretching worldwide with more than forty thousand child actors and just plain children auditioning for the role that would most certainly change their lives.

Joanne acknowledged that finding an actor to

play Harry was proving difficult and that finding an actor with the right look and acting ability was a challenge equivalent to the search that led to the choice of actress Vivian Leigh to play Scarlett O'Hara in *Gone With The Wind*.

"We'll know him when we find him," she said to *Newsweek*. "I am now walking around in London and Edinburgh, and I'm looking at kids as I pass them, just thinking, Could be, you never know. I may just lunge at this kid and say, 'Can you act? You're coming with me. Taxi.' "

Initially, the movie studio had hoped to get *Harry Potter and the Sorcerer's Stone* into theaters by summer 2001. But the combination of casting delays, lining up the incredible array of special effects and production design people necessary to bring the world of Harry Potter to the screen, and finding numerous London locations forced Warner Bros. to push back the release of the film to November 2001.

Casting the film was an ongoing challenge. Name actors as well as unknowns were being suggested for all roles. But midway through the year

2000, and a mere ten weeks before the start of filming, no actors had been cast.

Casting Harry continued to be the number one priority. More than eighty thousand letters went out soliciting actors to audition and the casting directors visited more than two hundred schools and numerous school drama departments. But the perfect Harry continued to be elusive.

Finally, on August 21, 2000, it was announced that eleven-year-old Daniel Radcliffe had been selected to play the coveted role of Harry Potter. The young British actor, who had previously appeared in the film biography of David Copperfield and the soon-to-be-released drama, *The Tailor of Panama,* was the spitting image of Harry Potter.

Joanne was ecstatic when she saw the youngster's screen test, feeling that after a long search, they had found their Harry. Director Chris Columbus was likewise thrilled.

"We saw so many enormously talented kids in the search for Harry," he said in an announcement on the Harry Potter Web site. "The process was intense, and there were times when we felt we would never find an individual who embodied the complex spirit and depth of Harry Potter. Then Dan walked into the room and we all knew that we had found Harry."

Radcliffe was officially presented as the film's Harry Potter in an August press conference. The youngster took easily to his new life in the spotlight as he patiently answered the media's questions.

"I cried and I was really excited," he said, in a *Hollywood Reporter* story. "I think I'm a tiny bit like Harry because I'd like to have an owl. I am looking forward to filming."

At the press conference, it was also announced that, since the movie would be titled *Harry Potter and the Sorcerer's Stone* in the United States and *Harry Potter and the Philosopher's Stone* in the rest of the world, a total of seven scenes would be shot two different ways to allow for dialogue to include references to both titles.

Also cast as Harry's closest friends were ten-year-old Emma Watson as Hermione Granger and eleven-year-old Rupert Grint as Ron Weasley.

With the core trio of roles now cast, the remainder of the all-important supporting characters quickly fell into place.

They were: Sean Biggerstaff (Oliver Wood), David Bradley (Argus Filch), John Cleese (Nick The Nearly Headless Ghost), Robbie Coltrane (Hagrid), Alfie Enoch (Dean Thomas), Tom Felton (Draco Malfoy), and Richard Griffiths (Uncle Dursley). Also cast were Richard Harris (Professor Dumbledore), Ian Hart (Professor Quirrell), Joshua Herdman (Gregory Goyle), Matt Lewis (Neville Longbottom), Rik Mayall (Peeves The Poltergeist), Devon Murray (Seamus), Katharine Nicholson (Pansy Parkinson) and Chris Rattling (Percy Weasley). Filling out the cast were Alan Rickman (Snape), Fiona Shaw (Aunt Petunia), Maggie Smith (Professor Minerva McGonagall), Verne Troyer (a ghoul), Zoe Wannamaker (Madame Hooch), Julie Walters (Mrs. Weasley), and Jamie Waylett (Vincent Crabbe).

Harry Potter and the Sorcerer's Stone began filming in mid October 2000. It was cold in London as the cameras rolled for the first time. So cold that, when not shooting in the relative comfort of Leavesden Studios, heavy coats and hot water bottles were the order of the day.

As Joanne would find during her many visits to the set, her fears that Hollywood would do something bad to her story were unfounded. Under director Chris Columbus's direction, London locations as diverse as Christ Church College, the reptile section of the London Zoo, Oxford University, the famed Australia House and Durham Cathedral had been magically transformed into delightful, larger-than-life landmarks of the Harry Potter world.

Throughout the production, Joanne would constantly, by telephone, E-mail, and fax, be kept abreast of any last-minute script changes, casting additions, and the film's progress in general. She happily reported to *Entertainment Weekly,* "They [Warner Bros.] have been very gracious in allowing me input and I have been asked a lot of questions I never expected to be asked."

Typical of the attention to detail involved in the filming process was the day at King's Cross Station, where Harry boards The Hogwarts Express for his fateful trip to The Hogwarts School. A steam engine made to look like Joanne's fantastic creation sat idling on the track, awaiting Harry's leap of faith through the platform barriers. On either side of The Hogwarts Express were trains filled to overflowing with extras. Packed together on the platform were hundreds of child extras, many of them dressed in true-to-life Hogwarts uniforms, while others were wearing felt hats and cloaks. Scattered around the platform were luggage trolleys piled high with bags, trunks, and broomsticks.

Amid the clutter of cameras, cables, and crew people, director Columbus carried on an animated conversation with Daniel. There were smiles and laughs between them as Columbus instructed the actor on where to walk and how to look so he would be in the camera frame. Finally, the director called for action and the complex sequence of moving extras, trains, and all manner of technical challenges unfolded in one continuous take as Harry approaches the train and makes the life-changing decision to step aboard. The scene required a number of takes and the better part of a day to get right, but as the cast and crew wrapped up filming for the day, this important sequence was in the can.

Screenwriter Kloves, a frequent visitor to the *Sorcerer's Stone* set, came away with hints of other great moments. He claimed that sequences involving the flying broomsticks were "amazing" and that scenes featuring Hagrid looked "cool."

Reports would continue to filter out of the top-secret production—that the actors were doing an excellent job of bringing Joanne's creations to life and that the production designers and special effects people had made literal magic in bringing the Harry Potter universe to the screen. Joanne was heartened by the fact that her hopes for the film were finally being rewarded.

But the fantasy of filming *Harry Potter and the Sorcerer's Stone* occasionally ran afoul of reality. Much of the movie was being shot in the middle of England's often wet winter, and so the moviemakers would frequently have to shut down for the day because of rain. There were also some anxious moments when, because of his age and the laws regarding child actors, it was determined that, because of the delays, Daniel might not be able to finish the film. But after some careful negotiations, everybody had smiles on their faces and Daniel would be allowed to finish the movie.

The advance word on the film was so good that the movie studio announced that they had already approved the script for *Harry Potter and the Chamber of Secrets* and that filming of the second movie would begin before the end of 2001.

While *Harry Potter and the Sorcerer's Stone* would continue filming throughout the winter and into the summer months in London, Joanne was home in Edinburgh. Hard at work.

Joanne had never really had a timetable for completing any of her books in the early stages of her publishing career; instead, with few distractions, she had been able to complete the first books in the Harry Potter series in just about a year. But, as the worldwide popularity of the books developed and the demand for her time increased, Joanne was admittedly having a hard time conforming to her normal writing schedule. Plus, in the back of her mind, she felt that taking the extra time might help avoid the delays and errors that plagued *Harry Potter and the Goblet of Fire*.

And so while she had hoped to have the fifth Harry Potter book out in time for the November 21, 2001, release of *Harry Potter and the Sorcerer's Stone*, midway through the year, Joanne would have to admit that she was not going to be able to complete the book. Her original goal had been to have Harry leaving Hogwarts as a full-fledged seventeen-year-old wizard in 2003. But now that goal has been put in doubt.

Because there would not be a Harry Potter book in 2001.

12

INTO THE FUTURE

Word quickly spread around the world that *Harry Potter and the Order of the Phoenix* would not be published until sometime in 2002.

Fans were disappointed and more than a little bit frustrated at the prospect of having to wait more than a year for their next Harry Potter adventure. So were Joanne's publishers, who had been hoping to make a big splash with the new Harry Potter book coming out at the same time as the movie version of *Harry Potter and the Sorcerer's Stone*. And her publishers did put some pressure on her to try and meet the original timetable for the new book.

But Joanne stood her ground and refused to rush things.

"I really want to take my time and just make sure that it's as good as I can make it," she told a Knight Ridder News Service reporter. "I don't want to be running up against an artificial deadline. I'm working on it now and I have no intention of taking a break."

To those familiar with Joanne's writing habits and attention to detail, it did not come as too much of a surprise that *Harry Potter and the Order of the Phoenix* was lagging behind schedule. Despite the fact that Joanne had long ago plotted out the seven books of Harry Potter, she had always prided herself on her ability to restructure the story and play with elements of her characters to the point where she was finally satisfied. Consequently, it took a year or more to complete each of the first four Harry Potter books.

But according to close acquaintances, Joanne

was suffering a bit of writer's fatigue based partly on the fact that she had, in hindsight, objected to the level of hysteria and secrecy surrounding the release of *Harry Potter and the Goblet of Fire*. In the aftermath of that experience, she was afraid that she would stop enjoying the writing process if she did not take a break and have a normal life.

So for a while, Joanne took things a little easier. She continued to write on a daily basis, but rather than pushing on when she became tired or distracted as she had in the past, she would stop writing. Joanne would often take leisurely walks through the city, or make time to be with her daughter and with family and friends. This less hectic approach to writing agreed with her, and Joanne would eagerly return to Harry each day with a new sense of excitement.

Now that it was common knowledge that Joanne was working on the fifth Harry Potter adventure, the curiosity began once again to grow. Jessica would often return from school and tell her mother that the children were pestering her with questions about what *Harry Potter and the Order of the Phoenix* was all about. And it was a favorite topic of conversation in the handful of interviews Joanne did during this period.

Not surprisingly, Joanne has refused to give away too much information about the story line of book number five. But she has indicated that *Goblet of Fire* was the end of an era in Harry Potter's life and that *Harry Potter and the Order of the Phoenix* will point Harry's life in a totally different direction.

She hinted to the *New York Times* that Harry's "innocence is gone," that "the mood may darken," and that the death in book four is "the beginning of the deaths" that may continue in the next book. She also hints that in book five readers will discover why Harry returns to the Dursleys each summer and that Ginny Weasley, who had a crush on Harry in *Goblet of Fire,* will play a bigger role in the adventure. She also good-naturedly predicts that *Order of the Phoenix* will be scary, and that "Harry finds out a lot of things he hasn't stumbled across so far."

"Harry has already dealt with death," she told a Canadian Broadcast Corporation interviewer. "He lost his parents very young and in book four

he witnessed a murder. So this is not news to anyone who has been following the series, that death
is a central theme of the books. It would be fair to
say that in book five he has to examine exactly what
death means in closer ways. But I don't think people who have been following the series will be that
surprised by that."

She also warned readers that book five will see
Harry's horizons broadening, and that he will be
entering totally new areas of his magical world.

But while *Harry Potter and the Order of the
Phoenix* would not come out for a while, there
would be some new Harry Potter–related books.
Midway through 2000, Joanne came up with an
idea to help fund one of her favorite charities,
Comedy Relief U.K. She agreed to write two 64-
page books, both under a pseudonym, based on
titles that appear in the Hogwarts library, with all
proceeds from sales going to Comedy Relief's
Harry Potter Fund, which was formed with
Joanne's cooperation to help fund children's
causes.

The first book, *Quidditch Through the Ages,* is
a fanciful, comprehensive guide to Quidditch and

a resource guide to the magical world and its most popular sport. For this book, Joanne took the name Kennilworthy Whisp. The second book, *Fantastic Beasts and Where to Find Them,* is an A-to-Z listing of all the fantastic creatures that populate the world of Harry Potter. Joanne wrote this book under the name Newt Scamander.

"I have always wanted to write these two books," Joanne said in a press release announcing the books. "I thought it was a wonderful opportunity to be involved in a charity I have always supported."

Word quickly spread throughout Harry Potter fandom and the books were immediately snapped up upon their release in early 2001. Joanne would happily report that millions of dollars made from the sales of the two books had made their way into the Harry Potter Fund.

Joanne continued to use her writing for good works when she agreed to pen an original short story for a short-story collection—which will be published in 2002—that will raise money for the National Council for Single Parent Families. Little is known about Joanne's contribution except that

Harry Potter would not be in it and that its story, in keeping with the theme of the book, would be about some element of magic.

As 2001 came to an end, Joanne would plan to enjoy the holidays close to home and with family and friends. Christmas would see Joanne and Jessica enjoying a huge dinner with her sister and her family; a highlight would be watching her brother-in-law, a chef, cook up the holiday turkey. New Year's would see Joanne and her daughter on holiday, taking in the sights and relaxing away from the constant demands on her time.

With her sister, Di, her family, and her close-knit circle of friends, Joanne could be assured of being treated as something other than a celebrity author. To these people, she was simply Joanne and that was fine with her. Because, in her heart, Joanne was basically a shy personality who was still coming to terms with the celebrity status that Harry Potter had brought her—to a large extent taking her away from the quiet life she had known. And while she now realized that she would forever be in the public eye, there was still a part of her that craved the privacy of a low-profile life.

After the first of the year, Joanne would return to the reclusive life of a writer, insulating herself from outside distractions as she continued to work on *Harry Potter and the Order of the Phoenix*. She was once again excited as the adventure continued, first in her mind and then on the page, at a steady pace. For Joanne, writing *Order of the Phoenix* was a welcome return to the quiet times she had experienced before her simple tales of Harry Potter had catapulted her into the spotlight.

But she could not completely hide from the notoriety that goes along with the fact that *Harry Potter and the Goblet of Fire* sold nearly 3 million copies in its first week and that there were nearly 50 million copies of her books in print in the United States alone. She has said that she has no idea if the worldwide mania for Harry Potter has reached its peak, and she is not sure if, even after four books, she has learned how to deal with the fame.

"I'm still learning," she told a group of reporters while in Canada. "I would definitely not say I'm on top of it. I would say that for the first two years of it, I was in denial. I kept thinking, 'It will go away.' And about the time of the publishing of the third book, I had to accept the fact that it wasn't going away any time soon, which is probably a healthier place to be. It will go away. That's the nature of the game. And when it does I believe I will be happy. And I will have fond memories of the time I was famous."

And the financial security that her fame has brought her. Joanne recently bought a second home in London, but anyone expecting her to spend her money frivolously on cars and helicopters, as was once speculated on in *Newsweek*, is sadly mistaken.

"Well, I can't drive so the five cars would be a problem," she laughingly explained in response to *Newsweek*'s question. "I don't want anyone thinking I'm a puritan. I enjoy spending money. But the main difference between where I was five years ago and now is the absence of worry. I honestly believe that the only people who will really appreciate that are people who have been very, very broke. What I'm grateful for every day is that I'm not worried about the money."

Money has always been a rather sticky subject

with Joanne. It has been speculated often in newspapers and magazines about how much Joanne has made and how rich she is. Joanne has often refused to put an actual number to her riches. But she did recently state in a *Philadelphia Inquirer* interview that "I could not write anymore and never have to worry about not having money again."

Joanne's notoriety and generous contributions to local charities have done much to make the author an unofficial ambassador for England and a favorite of the Royal Family. Early in the year 2001, Joanne was invited to their Gloucestershire country home for a meeting with Prince William, in which the heir to the throne complimented her on her books and her devotion to charity. On March 22, she was delighted and quite humbled when she had an audience with Queen Elizabeth on the occasion of a meeting between the Queen and members of the British publishing industry.

It was also during this time that Joanne fell in love.

Not much was known about how the couple met or who the man was, but what was known was that whenever spotted walking hand-in-hand on the streets of Edinburgh, they seemed deliriously happy. Personally and professionally, Joanne appeared to be in a state of grace.

In terms of her chosen profession, she also considered herself very lucky.

"It [writing] has made me happier," she said in a *Newsweek* interview. "Finishing them [the books] has made me happier. It also makes me happy that the one thing I thought I could do, I wasn't deluded."

And she was now looking to the future.

Uppermost in her mind was the future of the remaining books in the Harry Potter odyssey. Speculation is that book six will be titled *Harry Potter and the Green Flame Torch,* a rumor Joanne would deny. What she would speculate on was that she sees the remaining books as an exploration of the many personal and magical elements of Harry's character as he moves through his teen years. She sees the possibility of a romantic relationship for Harry and a more realistic interaction with the world around him. And while the final adventure of Harry Potter is still a few years off, Joanne is already looking forward to that finale.

"Book seven will be the biggest," she predicted in a *Newsweek* interview. "Seven is going to be like the *Encyclopaedia Britannica* because I'm going to want to say good-bye."

How she ultimately chooses to end the odyssey of Harry is still a mystery. Although she has acknowledged that she has already written the last chapter to the last book, doing so was mostly an act of faith to show that she really will get there in the end. Joanne is not quite sure what leads up to that moment. "Besides I might just end up rewriting that chapter," she joked during an online chat.

But, she offered the *Philadelphia Inquirer*, certain emotional elements of the final Harry Potter book are already in place. "By the series end you feel a sense of resolution. You find out what happens to the survivors, to those characters who live through all seven books. I know that sounds very ominous."

In the coming months, Joanne will remain the authority on her world as she oversees the completion of the movie version of *Harry Potter and the Sorcerer's Stone* and checks her E-mail regularly for missives from screenwriter Steven Kloves, who is already hard at work on the script for *Harry Potter and the Chamber of Secrets.* In fact, Warner Bros. has recently finalized a deal for the film rights to all seven Harry Potter books, which means that long after Joanne has written the literal last word on Harry, her legacy will be on the screen well into the next decade.

But with the self-imposed end of Harry Potter now in sight, Joanne looks at her creation with mixed emotions. "I think when I've finished the seven Harry Potter books, I will be finished with the world," she ventured in a Barnes & Noble on-line chat. "It will make me very sad to say good-bye, but it must be done."

Of course there were the rumors. The world-wide success of the Harry Potter books had been so massive that, reportedly, Joanne's publishers were hinting that it would be great if Joanne took Harry out of Hogwarts and into the world as a full-fledged wizard. Although Joanne would publicly laugh off the notion of carrying Harry's adventures further than the projected seven books, she would occasionally tantalize a reporter with the notion that yes, indeed, there were still stories that could be told.

"I always said there would be seven," she said in an America Online chat. "If there's ever an eighth, it will be because, ten years down the line, I had a burning desire to do just one more. But I don't presently think that will happen. However, I think I might write a kind of 'Harry Potter Encyclopedia' and give the royalties to charity."

And she indicated in the same chat that the notion of continuing to write children's books was also a possibility. "I might write more children's books. I really don't know. I should say, however, that I do not feel I have to write my 'serious' adult book to be a 'proper' author. The idea comes first, not the target audience."

Harry Potter and the Sorcerer's Stone was scheduled to complete filming in the summer of 2001. Joanne, during her periodic visits to the filming, had been impressed and amazed at how her world was being translated from the page to the screen. The excitement continued into the fall as the publicity machine for the film switched into high gear.

Everywhere she turned, she saw Harry or selected images from the film. The film studio was being cautious not to overpublicize the movie, but the early reaction to the bits and pieces of the film that were made available in movie theaters and on television created an excitement around the coming movie that easily rivaled the arrival of each new Harry Potter book. As the days counted down to the November release of the film, Joanne could not help but find herself anticipating the movie, right along with her fans.

It was a good feeling.

"I'm going to be sitting there like everybody else, really wanting to watch Quidditch," she told CNN interviewer Larry King. "That's the thing I want to see most. I've been watching this inside my head for ten years so to be able to physically watch it on the screen. I feel like a kid when I think about it."

ABOUT THE AUTHOR

Marc Shapiro has been a freelance entertainment journalist for more than twenty-five years, covering film, television, and music for a number of national and international newspapers and magazines. He is the author of more than a dozen celebrity biographies, including *Freddie Prinze Jr.: The Unofficial Biography, Love Story: The Unauthorized Biography of Jennifer Love Hewitt*, and *Lucy Lawless: Warrior Princess*. He lives in Pasadena, California, with his wife, Nancy, daughter, Rachael, dog, Keri, and cats, Bad Baby and Chaos.